Baed

San Francisco

Contents

The Principal Places of Tourist Interest at a Glance

Preface

This guide is one of the new generation of Baedeker guides.

Illustrated throughout in colour, they are designed to meet the needs of the modern traveller. They are quick and easy to consult, with the principal places of interest described in alphabetical order, and the information is presented in a format that is both attractive and easy to follow.

The subject of this guide is mainly the city of San Francisco, but it also includes places worth seeing in the surroundings such as Carmel, Monterey, the Napa Valley and the Yosemite National Park.

The guide is in three parts. The first part gives a general account of San Francisco, its population, economy, transport and culture; its history and famous people. A selection of quotations provides a transition into the second part, in which the places and features of tourist interest are described. The third part contains a variety of practical information. Both the sights and the practical information are listed in alphabetical order.

The new Baedeker guides are noted for their concentration on essentials and their convenience of use. They contain numerous specially drawn plans and colour illustrations; and at the end of the book is a large map making it easy to locate the various places described in the "A to Z" section of the guide with the help of the co-ordinates given at the head of each entry.

How to use this book

Following the tradition established by Karl Baedeker in 1844, sights of particular interest, outstanding buildings, works of art, etc., as well as good hotels and restaurants are distinguished by either one ★ or two ★★ stars.

To make it easier to locate the various sights listed in the "A to Z" section of the Guide, their co-ordinates on the large city map are shown in red at the head of each entry, e.g. ★Fisherman's Wharf H7.

Only a selection of hotels, restaurants and shops can be given; no reflection is implied, therefore, on establishments not included.

The symbol ⓘ on a town plan indicates the local tourist office from which further information can be obtained. The post-horn symbol indicates a post office.

In a time of rapid change it is difficult to ensure that all the information given is entirely accurate and up to date, and the possibility of error can never be completely eliminated. Although the publishers can accept no responsibility for inaccuracies and omissions, they are always grateful for corrections and suggestions for improvement.

Facts and Figures

Arms of the
City of
San Francisco

General

San Francisco is situated in the far west of the USA, on the Pacific
seaboard (city centre 37°45′10″N, 122°26′27″W). It is the fourth largest
city in the state of California after Los Angeles, San Diego and San
José, which overtook it a few years ago, and the fourteenth largest in
the United States.

Situation and
Importance

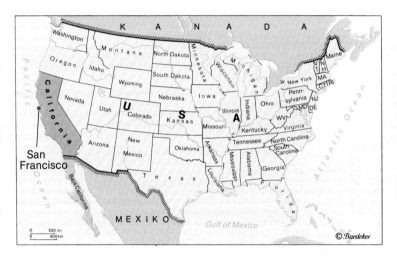

Greater San Francisco covers a total surface area of 128sq.miles/
332sq.km, of which nearly two-thirds is water, and takes in the Californian counties of Tuolumne, San Mateo, Kern, Fresno and Monterey.
   The actual city of San Francisco, which includes the out-lying counties of Marin in the north, San Mateo in the south and Alameda and
Contra Costa in the east, has a population of about 740,000.

Area and
Population

The city has a central administration which is headed by a mayor who
comes up for election every four years.

Administration

The mayor is aided by a chief executive administrator, the counterpart,
albeit with lesser powers, of the City Managers found in many other
American cities. The Board of Supervisors, the equivalent of a single
chamber for local government, consists of eleven elected members.

The city's current constitution dates from 1931 but has been subject to
over 400 amendments which makes it some 110,000 words long.

◀ *City of hills – Powell Street in downtown San Francisco*

Population

Population

The population of San Francisco originally grew very slowly and in 1846, which saw the end of Mexican rule, amounted to barely a thousand, dropping to a few hundred in the years immediately following – in 1847 San Francisco had a population of 459 which included 22 English, 27 Germans, 14 Irish, 14 Scots, 228 native-born Americans and 89 "Californians".

The 1849 Gold Rush sparked off a population explosion. Within a year numbers had risen to an estimated 25,000 and by 1890 stood at almost 300,000. Having reached 342,000 in 1900, they fell away sharply to 175,000 following the earthquake in 1906. By 1910 however the population had more than recovered to 416,000. In 1920 it had grown to 506,000 and in 1950 peaked at 775,000. The last 35 years have seen a decline of about 100,000, owing primarily to people moving out of the city to live in the surrounding countryside. The 1980 census recorded a total population of 679,0000, the lowest since 1950, the number of whites having plummeted disproportionally from almost 700,000 in 1950 to less than 450,000. In 1994 the total population was 724,000. Whites form the largest group, followed by blacks and Chinese. There are also e.g. Filipinos, Japanese, Indians, Koreans, Samoans, and Malaysians. The percentage of Asians is higher in San Francisco than in any other American city.

Ethnic variety

Quite apart from the many Asians, the people of San Francisco hail from a host of different ethnic backgrounds. The Chinese make up the largest ethnic group (13%), followed by blacks (11.3%), English (10.3%), Irish (8.5%), Germans (7.5%), Italians (5.7%), Filipinos (5.5%), Mexicans (5.3%), Russians (2.8%), French (2.5%) and Japanese (2.3%).

San Francisco even has a small Russian enclave around Clement and Geary Streets, while most blacks live in the area of Western Addition. Another indication of the city's unusually broad ethnic mix is the extraordinary cosmopolitan range of its restaurants.

Gays

Gays form one of San Francisco's most prominent, as well as militant, minorities, being well-organised and politically very active. When in 1978 the mayor of the time and the city's first homosexual Supervisor were gunned down by an aggrieved ex-colleague who was then given a relatively light sentence, the city erupted in days of rioting which subsided only when the new mayor, Dianne Feinstein, nominated another gay to take the murdered Supervisor's place. A survey published at the end of 1984 showed 40% of San Francisco's single men to be homosexual. The rapid spread of AIDS – by 1987 about 70% of the city's gay community were found to be HIV positive – has had a profound effect on the homosexual scene. Fear of infection has come increasingly to influence the social climate while on the political front there are ever greater demands for further action to combat the disease and to fight discrimination against AIDS sufferers and those infected with the AIDS virus.

Cults and Movements

San Francisco was also in the forefront of change as the city in which the beatnik and hippy movement first took root before spreading elsewhere. It was also the breeding ground for more unsavoury phenomena such as the Symbionese Liberation Army and the sect led by the fanatical Jim Jones – violence has never been a stranger to this, the first major city to have sprung from the Wild West.

Religion

Like almost every city in the USA San Francisco boasts a multitude of different religions. It is the seat of a Catholic Archbishop, and of the Episcopalian Bishop for the whole of Northern California. Virtually

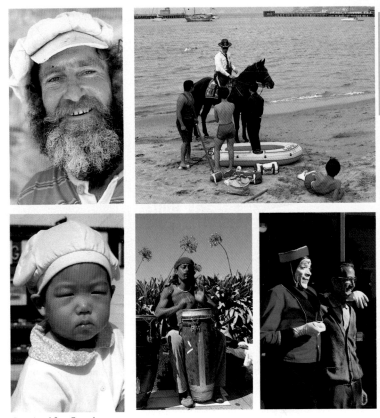

People of San Francisco

every religious denomination found in the United States has its places of worship here, including two Russian Orthodox cathedrals. The largest Lutheran congregation is that of St Mark's near St Mary's Cathedral. The city has long been a hotbed of religious sects, of which the most notorious was the People's Temple. Its leader, Jim Jones, succeeded in attracting a large number of idealistic followers, mostly from among the blacks and the poor, and led them on to mass suicide in Guyana. In the early 1970s Zen Buddhism gained its first foothold in the United States in San Francisco, due mainly to the writings of Alan Watts, a former Anglican priest and the most influential exponent of Oriental religions in the West.

Economy

Compared to Los Angeles with its oil industry and high degree of industrialisation, and also to other parts of Southern California, San Francisco has never been at the forefront as an industrial centre. It owes its importance much more to services and tourism.

Banking and Insurance

The business quarter – heart of commercial San Francisco

Foremost among its service industries are its banks, which include America's biggest bank, the Bank of America, as well as the Bank of California and the Wells Fargo Bank.

The city is also important for its insurance companies, to which it owes its newest landmark, the Transamerica Pyramid. In the Pacific Stock Exchange San Francisco has the principal trading exchange in the American West.

Tourism

San Francisco's many hotels and restaurants are of incalculable value to its economy. The city is such a magnet that every year it attracts five times as many visitors as the resident population; almost a third of these three million visitors come to attend conventions of one sort or another.

Industry

Once the foundation of San Francisco's economy, industry centred on the port has been declining for many years and is unlikely ever to recover its earlier importance; the same is true of the city's fisheries and canneries.

Many industrial corporations have their headquarters in San Francisco while their plants are located elsewhere in California. Among the largest are Chevron and McKesson. Crown Zellerbach, cellulose producers, have their head offices in Oakland. ·

Transport

Port

In San Francisco Bay the city possesses a fine natural harbour which, although at one time America's principal port trading with the Far East, has in recent years lost much of its earlier importance. Nowadays many of the 46 piers (on both sides of the Ferry Building) stand empty

Passenger ships in San Francisco harbour

or out of commission. Tonnage handled has dropped to 2.5 million tons a year and the number of vessels discharging cargo to only 850 a year. As long ago as 1969 the port of San Francisco was overtaken by Oakland on the other side of the bay, which has since increased its lead, handling predominantly container traffic. The San Francisco fishing industry has also declined considerably.

The airport, 15 miles/25km south of the city, was opened in 1927 as Mills Field. With its expansion the name was changed to San Francisco Airport and finally to San Francisco International Airport. Today it is one of the largest in the United States, serving over 25 airlines. There is another airport at Oakland on the east side of San Francisco Bay.

Airport

Rail transport has long ceased to be of much significance in San Francisco as in many other American cities. Today Southern Pacific has only one station catering for commuter traffic. The Amtrak trains that run along the Pacific Coast leave from Oakland, passengers getting there by shuttle bus from the Transbay Terminal.

Railways

San Francisco is served by a large number of local and long-distance bus lines and has two main bus stations – the Greyhound Terminal and the Transbay Terminal.

Bus services

The bus network, comprising 57 routes in all and serving virtually every part of the city, is San Francisco's principal form of public transport. Operated by the Municipal Railway Company tickets are transferable between the various elements of the MUNI system, which includes the streetcars (trams).

MUNI

San Francisco does not have an underground system as such but in 1981 the four streetcar lines running along Market Street were taken

BART subway

11

Cable car in Hyde Street – in the background, Alcatraz

below ground. They form part of the BART (Bay Area Rapid Transit) subway and surface rail system linking central San Francisco with the surrounding counties. BART's first line opened in 1972

There are 31 stations in all on the 75 mile/120km network, eight of them in San Francisco itself. The 3 mile/6km stretch beneath the waters of the bay separating San Francisco from Oakland is the longest of its kind in the world.

Streetcars, Cable cars

Apart from Philadelphia, New Orleans and the Californian capital Sacramento, San Francisco is the only city in the USA to have retained its trams (or streetcars as they are known in the States). It has five streetcar lines, part underground, and three cable car lines, the latter service dating back over 100 years.

Ferries

The ferries, which before the bridges were built provided the only means of crossing the Bay, have now largely ceased operation although passenger ferries still serve the Bay communities of Larkspur and Sausalito (from the Ferry Building) and also Tiburon (from Ferry Building), Angel Island and Alcatraz (from Fisherman's Wharf).

Highways

Except to the south where Highway 101 provides the fastest direct route to Southern California (the other main roads south are Interstate 280 and State Highway 1 along the coast), San Francisco relies upon bridges to link it with the rest of California.

Northbound, Highway 101 crosses the Golden Gate Bridge heading for Northern California, the North-western United States, and Canada, with Coastal Highway 1 branching off. Interstate 80 runs eastwards over the San Francisco-Oakland Bay Bridge, while Highway 92 crosses the San Mateo Bridge leading to State Highway 17 and Interstate 680 (south). Other major routes are State Highway 24 and Interstate Highway 680 (north), and Interstate 580 (east).

You are now entering San Francisico

Culture

Until about 1960 San Francisco was the undisputed cultural centre of California. Since then that honour has had to be shared with Los Angeles, five times its size.

Today San Francisco has four major theatres and a number of "little" theatres. It has its own opera and, in the San Francisco Ballet, America's oldest ballet company. Its Symphony Orchestra, founded in 1911, moved into the newly built Louise M. Davies Symphony Hall in the autumn of 1980.

The city also boasts several first-class art museums – the M. H. de Young Memorial Museum, the Asian Art Museum, the San Francisco Museum of Modern Art, and the Palace of the Legion of Honor – and an important Science Museum belonging to the California Academy of Sciences, as well as many special museums, cultural centres and similar institutions.

Every year in late April/early May an international film festival is held in the Palace of Arts and Science and the Castro Theater. Established in 1957 it was the first of its kind in America.

The two universities most commonly associated with San Francisco are in fact located in nearby Berkeley (the University of California) and Palo Alto (Stanford University). The University of San Francisco, founded in 1855 as St Ignatius College and situated in the city itself, is the oldest of the academic establishments in the area and is still run by the Jesuits.

Bird's-eye view of the University of San Francisco with St Ignatius Church

The University of California Medical Center, also in San Francisco, is another prestigious city institution. Privately founded in 1964 it incorporates the highly respected University Hospital. Other noteworthy colleges include the San Francisco State University and the San Francisco Art Institute.

History

Juan Rodriguez Cabrillo sails into what is now San Diego Bay and six weeks later sights in San Francisco Bay the Farallon Islands which have formed part of the city since 1872. **1542**

Sir Francis Drake becomes the first European to set foot on the coast of Northern California, probably landing on the opposite side of the bay from San Francisco in what is now Marin County. He christens the area "Nova Albion" and claims it in the name of Queen Elizabeth I. **1579**

Sebastian Rodriguez Cermenho lands in what is now Drake's Bay, on the Marin coast, calling it La Bahia de San Francisco. This is the first use of the name later given to the city. **1595**

The present San Francisco Bay is discovered by Gaspar de Portola and his troops travelling overland. Together with Father Junípero Serra, founder of the mission, Portola, later to be the first Governor of Spanish California, is leader of a "Holy Expedition" heading northwards from Sonora in Mexico. **1769**

A group of 250 Spanish soldiers and civilians, led by Juan Bautista de Anza, decide on the site for the San Francisco Presidio. **1776**
   Consecration of the first "Mission Dolores", originally San Francisco de Assisi.

Otto von Kotzebue, German captain of the Russian ship "Rurik", on a voyage of discovery, writes of the degrading treatment meted out to the Indians (the Ohlons, who have lived in the area since the 2nd millennium B.C., the Miwoks, Carquins and Santa Claras). Also on board, as ship's botanist, is Adelbert von Chamisso whose experiences in California are described in his "Travels around the World", 1836. **1816**

The Mexicans, having cast off Spanish rule in 1821, reject President Andrew Jackson's offer of $500,000 for San Francisco Bay. In the same year William Richardson, an English whaling captain married to a Mexican and a convert to Catholicism, founds the village of Pueblo Yerba Buena. **1835**

Yerba Buena now has a population of 350 made up of Americans, Indians, Dutch and Spanish. **1845**

War between Mexico and the USA. For a brief period from June 10th to July 9th California is an independent republic. On July 9th, following the capture of Los Angeles, 70 marines from the US frigate "Portsmouth" land in Yerba Buena, raising the Stars and Stripes in the village square. **1846**
   Three weeks later a ship arrives carrying 238 Mormons who, having set sail in search of their Promised Land, find themselves back in a different part of the United States, the country they were trying to leave.

On January 30th Yerba Buena's first American "alcalde" or mayor, Lieutenant Washington A. Bartlett, announces that the town, now with a resident population excluding military and naval personnel of 459, is to be known henceforth as San Francisco. **1847**

On January 24th while erecting a windmill for John Augustus Sutter at Coloma in the foothills of the Sierra Nevada, James Marshall finds **1848** gold, a discovery which sets the seal on the future of San Francisco. When news reaches the outside world prospectors set off in their thousands for San Francisco, now the gateway to the gold fields on the Sacramento River.

1850   San Francisco, its population having mushroomed to 25,000, becomes a fully-fledged city. A few months later California joins the Union as the 31st State.

1851   San Francisco, which two years earlier had been just a speck on the map, now ranks fourth in the United States in terms of shipping (behind Boston, New York and New Orleans).

Fire destroys much of the city but it is soon rebuilt.

1852   California's prospectors establish a record, producing $80m worth of gold.

1854   The city has no fewer than 20 theatres and 573 saloons – one saloon for every 60 inhabitants.

Lola Montez, former mistress of Ludwig I of Bavaria, takes the town by storm.

1859   The city adopts its present seal.

1860   Within a decade the population has risen to 56,000, a figure it took New York 190 years, Boston 200 years, and Philadelphia 120 years to achieve.

The clipper "Andrew Jackson" breaks all records by making the voyage round the Horn from New York to San Francisco in only 89 days.

1862   Opening of the telegraph line direct to New York.

1865   On October 9th, following smaller tremors, San Francisco suffers its first major earthquake. A second quake on October 23rd causes considerable damage in the city.

1867   San Francisco is the scene of anti-Chinese demonstrations.

1869   The Central Pacific Railroad completes the building of the line from the East Coast to San Francisco, an event enthusiastically celebrated in the city.

San Francisco as it appeared in an engraving of 1852

The decision is taken to build Golden Gate Park. San Francisco has 150,000 inhabitants (Los Angeles 5700). — 1870

On August 2nd the cable car, brainchild of Andrew Hallidie, makes its first trip along the 100-yard stretch of Clay Street between Kearny and Jones Streets. — 1873

Opening of the Pacific Stock Exchange. — 1875

The Southern Pacific Railroad completes the line from San Francisco to Los Angeles. — 1876
  500 unemployed workers demonstrate in front of City Hall calling on the mayor to provide jobs.

July sees the first serious rioting directed against the Chinese. A Citizens' Safety Committee restores law and order. — 1877

The American Speaking Telephone Company publishes its first San Francisco telephone directory. — 1878

The population of San Francisco is now 234,000 (Los Angeles 11,200). — 1880

10,000 trade unionists, including a large number from the Seamen's Union, founded in 1880, take part in the biggest labour parade yet seen in San Francisco. — 1886

John McLaren, an immigrant Scot, becomes Administrator of Golden Gate Park, a position he is to hold for 56 years until his death at the age of 94. His is the decisive influence in shaping the park. — 1887

A historic day when, for the only recorded time, snow covers the whole of San Francisco. — February 5th 1887

Golden Gate Park is the setting for San Francisco's first large-scale exhibition, the California Midwinter International Exposition. — 1894

Opening of the Ferry Building — 1898

A new city constitution comes into force municipalising the city's gas, electricity and water supplies. — 1900
  The population now stands at 342,000.

Fifteen new banks open within a month; the following year sees the founding of the Bank of America, destined to become the USA's biggest bank. — 1903
  President Theodore Roosevelt sends the first message via the new Pacific Cable from San Francisco to the Philippines.
  Another first is recorded when an automobile is driven all the way from San Francisco to New York, taking 63 days.

At 5.12am San Francisco is hit by an earthquake which initially causes less damage in the city than in neighbouring towns. But fires started by the quake and fanned by strong winds reduce three-quarters of the city's houses, hotels and businesses to ashes. A quarter of a million people are made homeless, finding temporary shelter in tents in the Presidio and the city parks. Rebuilding proceeds apace funded by more than $100m contributed from all over the States. — April 18th 1906

An epidemic of the plague takes several months to bring under control; the last plague-ridden rat is caught in October 1908. — 1907

Celebrations on Christmas Eve mark completion of the rebuilding of the city. Luisa Tetrazzini, San Francisco's most popular artiste, sings — December 24th 1910

City in ruins – San Francisco after the 1906 earthquake

before a crowd estimated at 250,000 in front of the Lotta Fountain on Market Street.

1911	Founding of the San Francisco Symphony Orchestra.
1912	James Rolph begins his nineteen-year spell as mayor, a record un-matched before or since. The first municipal streetcar line comes into operation in Geary Street.
1915	The great Panama-Pacific International Exposition opens in Lincoln Park a few months after the first ship to take the new route through the Panama Canal docks in San Francisco. Alexander Graham Bell makes the first transcontinental telephone call from New York to San Francisco.
1916	In the course of a longshoremen's strike a bomb explodes on the corner of Market and Steuart Streets during a citizens' Preparedness Day parade. Ten people are killed and forty injured. Two labour leaders, Tom Mooney and Warren K. Billings, are arrested, convicted and jailed. After more than two decades of public campaigning sustained by the belief that they had been falsely accused, the two are finally pardoned and released, having spent 22 years in jail.
1917	The main building of the San Francisco Public Library in the Civic Center opens for use.
1920	The first party convention to select a presidential candidate takes place in San Francisco. The Democrats nominate James M. Cox and Franklin D. Roosevelt for President and Vice-President but fail to win the election in November.
1921	San Francisco, population now 506,676, loses its place as California's largest city to Los Angeles (576,673 inhabitants).

1912   James Rolph begins his nineteen-year spell as mayor, a record un-matched before or since.

        The first municipal streetcar line comes into operation in Geary Street.

1915   The great Panama-Pacific International Exposition opens in Lincoln Park a few months after the first ship to take the new route through the Panama Canal docks in San Francisco.

        Alexander Graham Bell makes the first transcontinental telephone call from New York to San Francisco.

1916   In the course of a longshoremen's strike a bomb explodes on the corner of Market and Steuart Streets during a citizens' Preparedness Day parade. Ten people are killed and forty injured. Two labour leaders, Tom Mooney and Warren K. Billings, are arrested, convicted and jailed. After more than two decades of public campaigning sustained by the belief that they had been falsely accused, the two are finally pardoned and released, having spent 22 years in jail.

1917   The main building of the San Francisco Public Library in the Civic Center opens for use.

1920   The first party convention to select a presidential candidate takes place in San Francisco. The Democrats nominate James M. Cox and Franklin D. Roosevelt for President and Vice-President but fail to win the election in November.

1921   San Francisco, population now 506,676, loses its place as California's largest city to Los Angeles (576,673 inhabitants).

Opening of the M. H. de Young Memorial Museum in Golden Gate Park. Pictures of the Dempsey-Carpentier fight are flown from the East Coast to San Francisco in 48 hours 45 minutes.

President Warren Harding dies from a stroke in the Palace Hotel four days after arriving in San Francisco. — 1923

Introduction of regular mail flights between New York and San Francisco. — 1924

Opening of Mills Field as San Francisco's municipal airport. — 1927

Inauguration of a regular air service between San Francisco and Los Angeles. — 1928

The German airship "Graf Zeppelin" flies over San Francisco en route from Tokyo, landing at Los Angeles. — August 25th 1929

Ratification of the City Constitution still in operation today. Puccini's "Tosca" becomes the first opera performed in the War Memorial Opera House (Civic Center). — 1932

Dedication of the Coit Tower on Telegraph Hill.
Alcatraz Island becomes a state penitentiary. — 1933

Start of a longshoremen's strike lasting more than two months and leading, on May 25th, to a general stoppage which completely paralyses the city. — May 9th 1934

Introduction of a trans-Pacific airmail service from San Francisco. — 1935

Inauguration of a passenger air service between San Francisco and Honolulu. — 1936

The San Francisco-Oakland Bay Bridge opens to traffic. — November 12th 1936

Opening of the Golden Gate Bridge, designed and constructed by Joseph B. Strauss. Three months earlier ten workers had been killed when a girder collapsed. — May 27th 1937

Opening of the Golden Gate Exposition on Treasure Island. — 1939

The day after Japan declares war on the United States, San Francisco experiences its first blackout. — December 8th 1941

The evacuation is begun of Japanese residents of San Francisco to internment camps inland. — August 6th 1942

Opening of the Founding Assembly of the United Nations Organisation in the War Memorial Opera House, followed two months later by the signing of the original Charter. — April 25th 1945

Three days of rioting in the Alcatraz penitentiary leave two prisoners and three warders dead. — 1946

Japan's Prime Minister Yoshida signs the Treaty ending hostilities between his country and the United States in the War Memorial Opera House. — September 8th 1951

San Francisco International Airport (previously Mills Field) opens. — 1954

History

On June 21st, having been out of operation for two years, cable car services resume; repairs have cost $60m.

1984

The Democratic Party convention held in the new Moscone Center nominates Walter Mondale for President. Geraldine Ferraro becomes the first woman to be nominated for Vice-President. However the Democrats lose the November election.

Another (the sixth) attempt to get a law passed restricting the building of high-rise office blocks fails, 52% of the electorate voting against.

1985

The Nobel Peace Prizewinner, Mother Theresa, builds a convent in San Francisco.

1986

At the seventh attempt a proposal to restrict development in downtown San Francisco finally succeeds. Building starts will in future be limited to 475,000sq.ft in any one year.

Skyscrapers built in the early 1980s have already changed the face of downtown San Francisco. Now several new hotels alter the character of the district around Union Square. Some 16% of the city's available office space stands empty; for the first time rents are actually falling.

1987

The 50th anniversary of the opening of the Golden Gate Bridge is marked with great celebrations.

On October 17th, at 5.04pm, the city is struck by the worst earthquake (6.9 on the Richter Scale) since the 'quake of 1906. Although occuring during the rush-hour, relatively few people are killed. As well as San Francisco, Oakland, Santa Cruz and Silicon Valley suffer considerable damage. Sections of important highways, including the San Francisco-Oakland Bridge, threatened with collapse, are closed for lengthy periods.

1989

The suicide of a 38-year-old AIDS sufferer, the 900th suicide in the 55-year history of the Golden Gate Bridge, brings demands for tighter safety measures.

1991

Two new museums, the Friends of Photography (Ansel Adams Center) and the Museum of the City of San Francisco, open.

On October 20th the most catastrophic fire in recent American history breaks out in neighbouring Berkeley and Oakland. Complete districts with their many wooden houses are destroyed. Damage is estimated at $1.5m.

January sees the opening of the new building designed by the Swiss architect Mario Botta for the San Francisco Museum of Modern Art.

1995

Famous People

Listed here alphabetically are a selection of the men and women who, associated with San Francisco by birth, residence or death, have achieved national or international recognition.

Ansel Adams
Photographer
(1902–84)

Born in San Francisco the photographer Ansel Adams became well-known chiefly for his lucid and sensitive black and white photographs of the Yosemite National Park and other nature reserves mostly located in the western United States. In addition to a number of books featuring the Sierra Nevada and the Californian desert, he also published a manual of photography and a book about the Nisei (the Japanese born in California). Examples of his work are found in practically every US museum with a photographic collection and Ansel Adams prints command high prices at auction. He made his last home at Carmel and died in nearby Monterey.

David Belasco
Theatre director
(1859–1931)

David Belasco, one of the most important pioneers of the early American theatre, was born in the cellar of a house in Howard Street. Several years later his family moved to Canada; at the age of six he began his life in the theatre as a child actor with travelling roadshows. In 1880 he made a first, unsuccessful, attempt to gain a foothold in New York but subsequently achieved widespread fame as a playwright, director and producer; the theatre bearing his name still stands in New York today. He was noted as a producer of stage effects and scenery, and also for the discovery and nurturing of new talent – many of his protégés rose to stardom in the acting profession. Puccini modelled two of his operas – "Madame Butterfly" and "The Girl of the Golden West" – on stage plays by Belasco.

Luther Burbank
Plant-breeder
(1849–1926)

At the age of 26 Luther Burbank left Massachusetts for California where his three brothers were already established. Influenced by Darwin's ideas he experimented with producing new plant strains by cross-breeding. His success was such that he became a living legend in Santa Rosa, his home until his death. He developed no less than 40 new varieties of plums and damsons and ten new kinds of berries as well as new tomatoes, peas, maize, roses, lilies and poppies. His several books, which include a volume of memoires, testify to his extraordinary accomplishments.

James J. Corbett
World boxing
champion
(1866–1933)

James J. Corbett, the first world heavyweight boxing champion, began his career working in a San Francisco bank. It was in San Francisco, in 1892, that he won his world title, beating John L. Sullivan. He held the title for five years before losing it to Bob Fitzsimmons. His reputation for never striking a foul blow earned Corbett the nickname "Gentleman Jim".

Isadora Duncan
Dancer
(1878–1927)

Born in the house bearing a plaque to this effect on the corner of Geary and Taylor Streets, the famous dancer Isadora Duncan was brought up by her divorced mother. Interested in dance from an early age, she had had only a few ballet lessons before she developed her own theories and techniques running counter to those of classical ballet. Clad in flowing robes she sought to re-create the dance forms of ancient Greece.

Although her first apearance in the States – in Chicago in 1899 – proved a failure, in Europe she won enthusiastic acclaim. In 1904, with her elder sister Elizabeth, she opened a school in Berlin before making

Isadora Duncan   *Jack London*   *Levi Strauss*

Paris her permanent base. In 1905 she embarked on the first of her tours of Russia; while her disdain for the rules of classical dance found little favour there, her zest for improvisation met with greater approval. The Russians were particularly taken with her predilection for short dance pieces set to the music of Gluck and Chopin, which no one had previously considered suitable for interpretation by dance. In 1921 she opened a school in Moscow. Her American tours, of which the last was in 1922, were less successful. Her love affairs were eagerly seized upon by the press and the American public disapproved of her avowed sympathy for the emergent Soviet Union.

Sam Francis, who comes from San Mateo and studied at the University of California in Berkeley and the California School of Fine Arts (now the San Francisco Art Institute), is one of the foremost painters of the present time. His work is seen in all the museums of contemporary art. His paintings, most of them large abstracts, reveal a wealth of colour and a highly developed sense of space.

Sam Francis
Painter
(b. 1923)

Born in Yonkers, close to New York City, the poet Lawrence Ferlinghetti studied in Paris at the Sorbonne and arrived in San Francisco in the early 1950s. As author, bookseller and publisher, he had a profound influence on every aspect of the city's literary life. A poet of the Beat Generation, through his publishing centre, the City Lights Bookshop, he enabled the Beat poets to become more widely known outside California. In 1956, for example, he published Allan Ginsberg's first work, "Howl".

Lawrence
Ferlinghetti
Writer
(b. 1919)

His own poetry employs unusual speech rhythms, given emphasis by a highly individual form of typography ("Pictures of the Gone World", 1955; "Her", 1960; "Starting from San Francisco", 1961; "Routines", 1964; "An Eye on the World", 1967; "Open Eye", 1973; *et al*).

Robert Frost, the major American poet, is more usually associated with New England than the West Coast; but in fact he was born in San Francisco where his father worked as a journalist. Following her husband's death in 1885, his New England mother took the young Robert back east and, apart from three years in England (1912–15), he lived for the remainder of his life in the states of Massachusetts and Vermont.

Robert Lee
Frost
Writer
(1874–1963)

Frost was 40 before he published his first volume of poetry which, with its formal simplicity of language and feeling for the everyday life of New England folk, was an immediate success. Ten more volumes followed, as well as several rather less well received plays.

23

In 1978 San Francisco honoured the poet by dedicating the Robert Frost Plaza (at the meeting of California Street and Market Street). A large bronze tablet bears four lines of Frost's verse:

"Such was the life in the Golden Gate:
Gold dusted all we drank and ate.
And I was one of the children told
We all must eat our peck of gold".

Bret Harte
Writer
(1836–1902)

Like many other early Californians the short-story writer Bret Harte hailed from the East Coast. Born in Albany, the capital of New York State, he came to San Francisco as a seventeen year old in 1853 shortly after the start of the Gold Rush. He worked for a number of different publications before, in 1868, becoming editor of the new "Overland Monthly". Within three years he had made it one of America's most influential literary journals.

The second issue of the journal contained Harte's most celebrated work "The Luck of Roaring Camp" in which, as in his other short stories of that period, he sketched, with an almost brutal naturalism leavened with the occasional touch of dry humour, episodes from California's pioneering days.

The "Atlantic Monthly" then put him under contract for the astounding sum, for that time, of $10,000 a year; but his published work in the next eight years (up to 1878) did not reach the standard of his earlier writing. In 1878 he was appointed US Consul in Krefeld, Germany, later transferring to a similar post in Glasgow, Scotland. In 1885 he moved to London where he spent the last years of his life.

William Randolph
Hearst
Newspaper
magnate
(1863–1951)

William Randolph Hearst's father arrived in California on foot in 1850 from the Mid West; within a decade he had joined the ranks of San Francisco's nouveaux riches, acquiring several mines, including silver mines in Nevada. William Randolph, his only son, was thus San Francisco-born with the proverbial silver spoon in his mouth. At the age of 24 his father set him up as publisher of the daily "San Francisco Examiner", but it was from a base in New York that he built up his magazine and newspaper empire.

Hearst's publications were distinguished by sensational reporting and extreme patriotism; he also introduced comic strips into the daily press. Later he diversified into broadcasting and film as well as investing in land, all the while continuing to exploit his father's mines. He lived in great style, building a castle in San Simeon where he installed his mistress, Marion Davies. Orson Welles created a less than flattering memorial to Hearst in his film "Citizen Kane".

In 1974 Hearst's granddaughter Patricia (Patty) Hearst (b. 1954) was kidnapped by terrorists. Captured the following year by the FBI, in 1976 she was given a lengthy prison sentence for taking part in crimes committed by her kidnappers. She was pardoned in 1979.

Jack London
Writer
(1876–1916)

Born in San Francisco, Jack (John Griffith) London was the illegitimate son of a travelling astrologer and was brought up by his unloving mother and a devoted stepfather. In his mid teens he worked in a cannery and a jute factory before going to sea, after which he was for a time unemployed. When in 1896 gold was first struck in the valley of the Klondike River in Canada, he joined the hordes streaming north in search of a fortune.

A professed "unscientific socialist", he published his first story in 1898 and went on to write more than 40 novels – the best-known is probably "Call of the Wild" – and a host of short stories. On November 22nd 1916 at Glen Ellen, California he took his own life, aged 40.

Robert Strange McNamara was born in San Francisco, the son of a Scottish immigrant. Having graduated from high school in his home town, he spent time at a number of colleges and universities, including the University of California in nearby Berkeley, but after a brief period as assistant professor of economics (1940–43) left to work in industry. In 1948 he joined the Ford Motor Company, rising to become President of the famous American car manufacturer in 1960. A year later President Kennedy took him into his Cabinet as Defence Secretary. Utilising his business experience McNamara tried to make the US armed forces a more effective fighting machine, but found his measures impeded by the growing intensity of the war in Vietnam which he began by supporting but came in the end to oppose. He remained US Defence Secretary until 1968. From 1968 to 1981 he was President of the World Bank.

Robert S. McNamara
Economist
(b. 1916)

Born a poor farm boy in a small town in New York State, Leland Amanas Stanford became one of the richest and most powerful men in San Francisco, where he lived from his arrival at the time of the Gold Rush until his death. Stanford sold food and clothes to the prospectors, often being paid in gold. From these early beginnings he worked his way up to become President of the Central Pacific Railroad and later State Governor and Senator for California. He built a magnificent mansion on Nob Hill where the Stanford Court Hotel now stands. As a memorial to his only son, who died at the age of fifteen, he founded in 1887 Stanford College, now Stanford University, in Palo Alto, and also the Stanford University Museum of Art, which originally bore his son's name.

Leland A. Stanford
Businessman and politician
(1824–93)

Though born in San Francisco the crusading journalist Lincoln Steffens grew up in Sacramento, capital of California, where his family lived in a huge Victorian house (which later became the Governor's Mansion). Having applied unsuccessfully to enter the university at Berkeley, he studied in Europe. Thereafter he worked on several of America's best-known newspapers, making a name for himself as the enemy of corruption in American city politics. Following publication of his magnum opus, "The Shame of the Cities", in 1904, he travelled extensively in the States collecting further material. This brought him back to the city of his birth which, because of its corrupt administration, in which ostensibly "pro-labour" officials proved to be in the pocket of the capitalist bosses, was singled out for some of his most savage attacks. In 1927 he retired to Carmel and four years later published his autobiography, setting out his aims for social reform.

Lincoln Steffens
Journalist
(1866–1936)

Levi Strauss, the German immigrant responsible for the world-famous Levis, the jeans that have been made in San Francisco since 1850, came to America at the age of fourteen. Before setting out west on the three-month voyage round Cape Horn, he stocked up from the store run by two of his brothers in New York with various types of cloth and several bales of sailcloth for use on covered wagons. By the time he arrived in San Francisco he had sold the lot, apart from the sailcloth. Hearing a prospector complaining one day that the hard work caused his pants to rip, Strauss hit on the idea of having trousers made up from the tough sailcloth. These were an instant success and in 1853 Strauss and his brothers founded the firm that still bears his name.

The idea of reinforcing the pockets of the jeans with copper studs came from a local tailor who patented it jointly with Strauss in 1873. Instead of sailcloth Strauss later used serge from Nîmes in France because it was even more hard-wearing; this "serge de Nîmes" came to be called "denim".

Levi Strauss
Trader
(1829–1902)

Quotations

Eugene Burdick
American writer
(1918–65)

The City (San Francisco) is the central part of California. Everything belongs to it from the Techahapis in the South up to the line of Marin County. Above lies the North. The City, San Francisco, is a living miracle, a discovery, something made up and not quite true. Everyone within the orbit of the City "lives" there. People from Palo Alto, San José, Santa Cruz, Berkeley, Orinda, Piedmont, Atherton and Oakland always say to outsiders that they're from the City – I mean, from San Francisco . . .

There are three Californias – Northern, Southern and the City. Each one is made up of people come in from other States. But they don't simply come to California, they come to one of these three Californias.

Three Californias

Duke Ellington
American
Jazz musician
(1899–1974)

San Francisco is one of the great places for culture in the world . . . a really urbane community in the USA, a really cosmopolitan place, and over the years it's always been set to welcome anyone from anywhere.

Lawrence
Ferlinghetti
American poet
(b. 1919)

San Francisco looked like an island, with the white houses, a little like Tunis seen from the sea, with a whiff of the Mediterranean and not at all like a piece of America. But that was an illusion. It was in every sense the place where the West came to an end, the place where the frontier first got tamed.

Oskar Maurus
Fontana
Austrian writer
(1889–1969)

Were not the bridges alone something to wonder at . . . like the Brooklyn Bridge and the Golden Gate Bridge of Frisco? Its building of bridges was for Heinrich the most visible and most exalted triumph of the spirit of the New World and perhaps in times to come – he felt – that was the task of America, also between the peoples of the world, in their confused state of Babel, to build such bridges, swaying on gigantic cables, over enormous gulfs in origins and feelings and thoughts.

The Fire's Breath

Herbert Gold
American writer
(b. 1924)

While New York and Paris can't wait to become larger variations on Cleveland . . . San Francisco secretly remains the same.

Arthur Holitscher
Austrian writer
(1869–1941)

For many a year my thoughts will return to the city at the Golden Gate, to the wonderful fairytale city where in a tropical garden I for the first time saw the sun setting in breathtaking splendour over the Pacific in the limitless waters of the West. San Francisco has mastered its fate and I find myself in a city that has been born anew.

Johannes V.
Jensen
Danish poet
(1873–1950)

Anyone who has been in Frisco retains particularly fond memories of this beautiful, bustling city, which lay as the farthermost outpost on the frontier between two worlds, pampered by the sun, apparently itself unaware of the exotic aura of golden dreams woven around its name . . . Frisco arises anew. The best estimate is made of when to expect the next earthquake and homes are built accordingly; in the interval following every earthquake a new San Francisco is born.

The New World

A journalist asked me what I thought of the city (San Francisco) and I promptly responded that for me Bret Harte had made it hallowed ground. That was the truth . . . San Francisco is a mad city, largely inhabited by the wholly deranged, whose women are of remarkable beauty.

Rudyard Kipling
English writer
(1865–1936)

From Sea to Sea

San Francisco was a dream, a temptress of old; I knew the name, I loved the city, familiar to me since my first days as a reader. San Francisco was the ultimate Wild West, adventure itself, the haven of the prodigal son, the bank clerk on the run, the profligate and the unruly, a magnet for the bold, a new life for those that had gone astray, last hope of the poor and the oppressed..., for me a place where I devoutly wished to be.

Wolfgang
Koeppen
German writer
(b. 1906)

American Journey

How much you love or hate a city depends on what it means to you and how it treats you. I love San Francisco. To me it means many things, above all freedom . . . I love San Francisco because for me it's full of memories. San Francisco itself is art, above all literary art, and I recall to mind, with profound respect, the great writers that were born here or came here to write: Jack London, Mark Twain, Ambrose Bierce and George Sterling. Every block is a short story, every hill a novel. Every home is a poem, every dweller within immortal. That is the whole truth.

William Saroyan
American writer
(1908–81)

Monsieur Verdier, owner of the great department store "City of Paris" in San Francisco is a survivor of the earthquake and conflagration which destroyed three-quarters of the city. He was a young man at the time and retained a clear recollection of the catastrophe. He then lived through the reconstruction of the city, which in 1913 was still Asian in character, and its subsequent Americanisation. Thus he recalled three different San Franciscos. Us, we ourselves change in unchanging cities and our houses, the areas we live in, outlive us; American cities change far faster than the people who live in them and thus it is the people who outlive the cities. For us a city primarily means the past – for the American it stands first and foremost for the future and what they love about it is all that is yet to come, all that they can become.

Jean-Paul Sartre
French
philosopher
(1905–80)

Situations III

There has never been anything to parallel San Francisco nor will there ever be. Like the magic seed of the Indian juggler that sprouted, blossomed and bore fruit before the very eyes of the onlooker so San Francisco seems in one day to have accomplished the growth of half a century.

Bayard Taylor
American writer
(1825–78)

Thank God I'm out of Canada again and back in the ghastly USA. Los Angeles and Hollywood are the nightmarish zenith of my crazy, lonely tour. But San Francisco! It is and has everything . . . In Canada, five

Dylan Thomas
Welsh poet
(1914–53)

ours' flying away, you would never think that a place like San Francisco can exist. The glorious sunshine, the hills, the great bridges, the Pacific at the feet. Lovely Chinatown. Every race in the world.

H. G. Wells
English writer
(1866–1946)

The great calamity . . . left no one with the impression that it amounted to an irrecoverable loss. This afternoon everyone is talking about it but no one is in the slightest downcast . . . Nowhere is there any doubt but that San Francisco will rise again, bigger, better and after the very briefest of intervals.

The Future in America; a Search after Realities

A typical scene: mist envelops the Golden Gate Bridge ▶

San Francisco from A to Z

Alcatraz Island

Location
1½ miles/2.4km
north-east in San
Francisco Bay

Ferries
Pier 41 (Fisher-
man's Wharf)
Summer: daily
9am–5pm
Autumn–spring:
daily 9am–3pm

Advance booking
Tel. 546–2805

Self-guided tour
with walkman $21

A trip to Alcatraz, the former island penitentiary situated 1½ miles/2.4km north-east in San Francisco Bay, is one of the most intriguing excursions in the immediate vicinity of the city. Its first European visitor, the Spaniard Ayala, christened it Isla de los Alcatraces (Pelican Island) on account of the innumerable pelicans nesting on the bleak lump of sandstone.

Since there are no springs on the rocky, 12 acre/5ha islet, 135ft/41m high, it was presumably uninhabited in earlier times. The first building was a lighthouse, erected in 1853 at the time of the Californian gold fever when the number of ships in the foggy bay greatly increased. Soon afterwards it was fortified and during the Civil War (1861–65) served as a military prison. From January 1st 1934 until its closure in 1963, Alcatraz was the most notorious and feared state penitentiary in the USA. Escape was extremely rare even with the resources available to professional gangsters (Al Capone among them, detained here from the beginning of 1934 until 1938): any attempt was likely to end in drowning in the ice-cold waters of the Bay.

In the course of its 30-year existence the penitentiary housed a total of 1576 convicts, never more than 250 at a time despite there being 450 cells, each measuring about 10 × 4ft/3 × 1.5m, in the prison block. On occasion indeed convicts were outnumbered by guards, etc.

After the penitentiary was closed the island lay virtually forgotten for six years until taken over by Indian squatters. Their occupation lasted seven

Alcatraz Island – view from Hyde Street

years. Although the island has been open to visitors since 1973 only emergency repairs have been made to the run-down buildings.

Note: warm clothes are advisable when visiting the island; it is often shrouded in mist and the wind is almost always strong.

The Anchorage (Shopping and leisure centre)   H 8 (H 4)

The Anchorage is one of San Francisco's newest attractions. There are nearly 50 shops and restaurants on various levels, as well as a hotel in a delightful architectural setting.

The centre of the complex is an inner courtyard where buskers from all over the city perform in a mini-amphitheatre.

Location
Leavenworth St.

Buses
15, 19, 30, 32

Cable cars
59, 60

Angel Island State Park   H 32

Angel Island, 740 acres/300ha in area, lies north of the city in San Francisco Bay. In the course of the last hundred years it was used as a quarantine station for immigrants from Asia and as a coastguard station, becoming a prisoner-of-war camp and anti-rocket site during the Second World War.

The uninhabited island is now a municipal park where some 200 head of red deer roam free.

Motor vehicles are banned from the island which, with its pleasant cycle tracks and footpaths and large picnic areas is a favourite spot for excursions from the city.

Location
3 miles/5km north in San Francisco Bay

Ferries
Pier 43½ (Fisherman's Wharf)
Summer: daily
Autumn–spring:
Fri.–Sun.
to Ayala Cove

The Bank of America building dominates the skyline (see page 32)

Asian Art Museum of San Francisco

See Golden Gate Park

★Bank of America   I 8 (J 5)

Location
555 California St.

This skyscraper belonging to the world's largest private bank (with capital of about $30 billion) is 52 storeys high and rises 760ft/232m. Together with the Transamerica Pyramid it has radically altered San Francisco's townscape. Two eminent firms of architects, Wurster, Bernardi & Emmons and Skidmore, Owings & Merrill, with Pietro Belluschi as consultant, designed the building in 1969. The material used is reddish South Dakota granite.

The complex comprises a lofty tower with offices, a low banking hall, and an open piazza with a sculpture by Masayuki Nagare, beneath which is an auditorium. In all 7500 persons work in the building. Visitors and employees are carried to the top of the tower by 32 lifts.
     Located on the uppermost storey, commanding a magnificent view, is the Carnelian Room Bar (tel. 433–7500 after 3pm for reservations).

Bank of California   I 8 (J 4/5)

The buildings

Location
400 California St.

The Bank of California is the oldest bank on the West coast. Its buildings in San Francisco have always been noted for their architectural merit.

Old and New in delightful harmony – the head office of the Bank of California

The first, erected in 1867 on the site occupied today by the Bank's latest shrine to Mammon, was Neo-Renaissance in style and was pulled down just before the earthquake of 1906. The second, which still stands on the corner of Sansome Street, took the form of a Corinthian temple, with pillars of California granite on two sides.

Rising alongside it, at 420 California Street, is the bank's most recent head office. Constructed in 1967, great importance was attached to preserving and harmonising with the earlier grey granite building. The "Museum of Money of the American West" (see below) is housed on the lower floor. Visitors never fail to be impressed by the dimensions of the bank's magnificent entrance hall (111 × 82 × 60ft/34 × 25 × 18m).

Marble from Tennessee was used. At one end there are statues of two mountain lions by the Californian sculptor Arthur Putnam.

Museum of Money of the American West

Although not very large, the Museum of Money of the American West is an important source of information on the history of the American West. Among the items on display are pieces of gold quartz from the time of the Gold Rush and nuggets of gold and silver, also a collection of gold coins and banknotes dating from the second half of the 19th c. Some of these were official issue, others produced by the banks themselves to cope with a shortage of coin during the period.

The museum's absorbing collection also includes weapons of historical interest, several of which were used by the participants in some notorious duels.

Location
420 California St.

Opening times
Mon.–Thur.
10am–3pm
Fri. 10am–5pm

Closed
Bank holidays

Entry free

Bay Bridge

See San Francisco–Oakland Bay Bridge

Benicia

Benicia (population 18,250; altitude 8ft/2.5m) is situated on the north shore of Carquinez Strait linking San Pablo Bay north of San Francisco to Suisin Bay. Founded in 1847 – even before California had joined the Union – Benicia is one of the oldest towns in the state. Although the hopes of its founders, to create a major harbour here, remained unfulfilled, Benicia was briefly capital of California, in 1853–54. It boasts the state's first Protestant church (built in 1859) and its first Free Masons Lodge. Worth visiting are the museum in the Capitol and the Historical Park on the shore of the strait south of the town. Other survivals from the early days include camel stables, a fine bell tower and a Dominican cemetery. Jack London was an oyster fisherman in Benicia.

Location
30 miles/50km
north-east
(Highway 80, 780)

★Berkeley

I 31

Berkeley lies some 12 miles/20km north-east of San Francisco, across the Bay. A city of 140,000 inhabitants, it retains its small town character despite its considerable amount of industry and its 45,000 students. Founded on ranchland in 1866, it was planned from the first as a university town. It is named after the Irish bishop and philosopher George Berkeley, responsible for the saying "Westward the Course of Empire takes its Way". In 1991 entire residential districts in Berkeley were destroyed by a catastrophic fire

Location
12 miles/20km
north-east
(Highway 80)

BART station
Berkeley

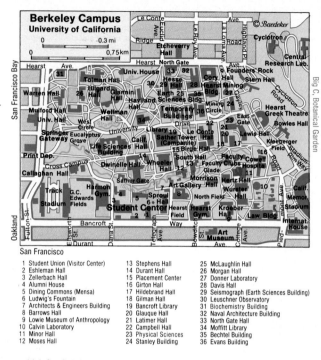

Berkeley Campus
University of California

1 Student Union (Visitor Center)
2 Eshleman Hall
3 Zellerbach Hall
4 Alumni House
5 Dining Commons (Mensa)
6 Ludwig's Fountain
7 Architects & Engineers Building
8 Barrows Hall
9 Lowie Museum of Anthropology
10 Calvin Laboratory
11 Minor Hall
12 Moses Hall
13 Stephens Hall
14 Durant Hall
15 Placement Center
16 Girton Hall
17 Hildebrand Hall
18 Gilman Hall
19 Bancroft Library
20 Glauque Hall
21 Latimer Hall
22 Campbell Hall
23 Physical Sciences
24 Stanley Building
25 McLaughlin Hall
26 Morgan Hall
27 Donner Laboratory
28 Davis Hall
29 Seismograph (Earth Sciences Building)
30 Leuschner Observatory
31 Biochemistry Building
32 Naval Architecture Building
33 North Gate Hall
34 Moffitt Library
35 Bechtel Building
36 Evans Building

which fire fighting precautions, introduced after a similar conflagration in 1923, proved powerless to prevent.

The main sights in the town are the Charles Lee Tilden Regional Park, and Bancroft Way with its places of amusement and shops frequented by the students. The principal attraction however is the world-famous University of California. Visitors to Berkeley can savour the unique atmosphere of an American university campus. An additional attraction is the University Art Museum with its collection of paintings by 19th and 20th c. artists and important film archive.

University of California

Location
Telegraph Avenue
and Bancroft Way

The University of California embraces the largest network of state higher educational establishments apart from the State University of New York. It oversees teaching in nine Californian cities. The Berkeley campus dates from the founding of a private college here in 1873. It is the oldest college in California and, with 45,000 students, the second largest after Los Angeles.
 The University of California is famous not only for its many Nobel Prize winners but also for being the source from which the student unrest of the 1960s spread throughout the Western World.

Guided tours

Mon.–Fri. 1pm, duration 1½ hours. Meet at the Students' Union (Visitors' Center). Booking essential for groups of more than five (tel. 510–642–5215).

Sather Tower – the symbol of the University of California at Berkeley ▶

Berkeley

Sather Tower
(campanile)

Opening times
daily
10am–4.15pm

Sather Tower, a campanile built in 1914, has long been the symbol of the university. Modelled on the tower of St Mark's in Venice, it stands more than 300ft/94m high, dominating the rest of the buildings on the extensive park-like campus. From the top (lift, 50 cents) there is a splendid view over the university, San Francisco Bay and the Golden Gate Bridge (see entry).

Note: visitors should try if at all possible to hear the carillon, rung on weekdays at 7.50am and 6pm (except at exam times), on Saturdays at 6pm and Sundays at 2pm.

Other buildings

The Tudor-style South Hall, the oldest building on campus (1873), stands south-west of the campanile. Farther south-west is Sather Gate which, with the Plaza, is the centre of student life.

The Earth Sciences Building, not far from the North Tower, houses palaeontological and mineralogical collections as well as an interesting seismograph on the first floor. The Chapel of the Pacific School of Religion (1198 Scenic Avenue; open to visitors Mon.–Fri. 8.30am–4.30pm) boasts one of the largest stained glass windows in the world.

Also noteworthy are the cyclotron (particle accelerator) in the north-east corner of the campus, and the California Memorial Stadium, a sports arena seating 76,500, in the south-east corner.

Lawrence
Berkeley
Laboratory

Another establishment of particular interest on campus is the Lawrence Berkeley Laboratory where Nobel Prizewinner Ernest O. Lawrence carried out his pioneering research in atomic physics. Among those working with him was Robert Oppenheimer, involved in fundamental research leading to the development of the first atomic bomb. Oppenheimer later opposed the making of the hydrogen bomb, giving rise in 1953 to an investigation into his alleged Communist sympathies. President Eisenhower banned him from any further participation in top secret projects.

Conducted tours of this rather special research laboratory take place on Tuesdays only, at 2pm (not public holidays or during the summer vacation). Application must be made in advance by telephoning 510–843–2740, extension 5611.

Museums

Among several interesting museums on campus, apart from the University Art Museum, are:

The Judah L. Magnes Memorial Museum, 2911 Russell Street, mainly devoted to a collection of Jewish ritual objects. There are two libraries associated with the museum (open: Sun.–Thur. 10am–4pm; tel. 510–849–2710).

The Palestine Institute, with a collection of archaeological finds from Palestine dating from Old Testament times to the 5th c. A.D. (open: daily 9am–5pm).

The Robert H. Lowie Museum of Anthropology (open: Mon.–Fri. 10am–4pm, Sat. and Sun. noon–4pm).

University Art Museum

Location
2626 Bancroft Way

Opening times
Wed.–Sun.
11am–5pm
Thur. entry free

Built in 1970 to designs by Mario Ciampi this museum on the university campus has won well-deserved acclaim in its few years in existence. Its collection is particularly extensive for a museum of such recent origin. This is because the university began acquiring works of art almost from its inception in 1873, later transferring them to the fledgling museum.

It was Hans Hofmann, a German painter active in America from 1932 onwards, who provided the decisive impetus to plans to build a museum here. Having taught for a while at Berkeley, in 1963 he presented the

Berkeley – the modern façade of Berkeley University Art Museum

university with 45 of his paintings, at the same time promising funds for a museum. Seven years later the buildings were ready. Nowadays about half the works Hofmann donated to the museum are displayed in one of its largest galleries. There is accordingly no better place to gain an appreciation of the painter's work. Among Hofmann's American pupils were Louise Nevelson, Helen Frankenthaler and Larry Rivers.

The museum also possesses a large collection of Oriental works of art and many 19th c. paintings. There are almost always several special exhibitions on at any one time, mainly focusing on the work of 20th c. painters, sculptors and photographers.

The museum is home to the Pacific Film Archive which always has an interesting programme of films showing in its 200-seat auditorium. It has a stock of 5000 movies, including the largest number of Japanese movies outside Japan itself. It also has many avant-garde and experimental US films and a collection of 35mm copies of Soviet silent films. (Performances: daily 7–11pm; tel. 510–642–1124 for programme information.)

Pacific Film
Archive

Bodega Bay

It was somewhere near this small bay, now part of the Point Reyes National Seashore (see entry), that Sir Francis Drake landed in 1597. In 1809 Ivan Kusko of the Russian-American Co. established a settlement on the bay with the object of growing wheat and trapping otters. To keep the Russians in check the Mexican governor, Vallejo, gave three American sailors land bordering the settlement. After the Russians left the land was sold to John A. Sutter. Nowadays Bodega Bay is a thriving fishing port. It was the location for Alfred Hitchcock's film "The Birds". The University of California has a marine laboratory here.

Location
65 miles/105km
north of San
Francisco

Buddha's Universal Church

See Chinatown

★★ Cable Cars   H–K 3–6

History

San Francisco is built on many hills and a major contribution to the city's development occurred in 1873 with the invention of the cable car. Since 1964 these tram-like vehicles have had the unique distinction of being the only public transport system to be declared a historic monument.

Andrew S. Hallidie was an Englishman who came to California at the time of the Gold Rush. He made steel cables for mining. In those days all transport was horse drawn and when in 1869 Hallidie witnessed a serious accident caused by a horse losing its footing on a slippery road, he conceived the idea of replacing the horse-drawn trams with a more modern system. On August 2nd 1873, after three years experimentation, he successfully demonstrated the first cable car in Clay Street.

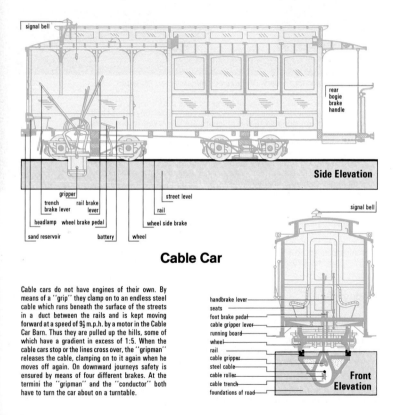

Cable Car

Cable cars do not have engines of their own. By means of a "grip" they clamp on to an endless steel cable which runs beneath the surface of the streets in a duct between the rails and is kept moving forward at a speed of $9\frac{1}{2}$ m.p.h. by a motor in the Cable Car Barn. Thus they are pulled up the hills, some of which have a gradient in excess of 1:5. When the cable cars stop or the lines cross over, the "gripman" releases the cable, clamping on to it again when he moves off again. On downward journeys safety is ensured by means of four different brakes. At the termini the "gripman" and the "conductor" both have to turn the car about on a turntable.

The cable cars – they cope with the city's steepest hills

The Cable Car Barn – control centre for the cable cars

His invention incorporated a moving cable running in a trench under the street, driven by huge wheels housed in specially constructed engine sheds or "barns". The "gripmen", as the drivers are called, lock the cars in position on the travelling cables; thus held fast they are able to cope with even the steepest of the city's hills. In 1890 there were no fewer than eight companies running cable car services, with more than 600 vehicles and over 100 miles/160km of track.

Cable cars today

Today there are just 40 cable cars operating on three surviving lines, forming a network only 10½ miles/17km in length. The cars proceed at a steady pace of 9½ mph/15kmph. Of the old barns only one remains. Most of the rolling stock still in service dates from the last century. Built of wood the cars seat 30–40 passengers but there are generally another 50 or so standing or strap-hanging.

In spite of numerous accidents the cable cars hold a special place in the hearts of San Francisco people. The city's constitution includes a clause forbidding discontinuance of the service. Between October 1982 and June 1984 the service was suspended for a long-overdue overhaul of the network and the cable cars themselves. The final cost was $60m of which all but $12m came from the state of California.

Cable Car Barn and Museum   I 4

Location
Corner of
Washington
and Mason St.

This red-brick building, erected in 1887, serves as the control centre for the three cable car lines still in operation. From an observation gallery it is possible to see just how the cable cars work. The system remains essentially unchanged since its invention in 1873.

In the museum visitors can examine three of the earliest vehicles which plied the route along Clay Street, also photographs and models of all the types of cable car ever put into service. There are continuous screenings of a film lasting quarter of an hour about cable cars and how they operate. Entry free.

Opening times   Apr.–Oct. daily 10am–6pm; Nov.–Mar. daily 10am–5pm.

Closed   Thanksgiving Day, Christmas Day and New Year's Day

California Academy of Sciences

See Golden Gate Park

California Historical Society (Museum)   G 8

Location
2090 Jackson St.

Bus
2 (to Laguna St.)

Opening times
Wed., Sat. and
Sun. 1–5pm
Entry free 1st
Sat. of month

Guided tours
Wed., Sat. and
Sun. 1.30pm

The California Historical Society is housed in Whittier Mansion, built in 1896 as a residence by a wealthy merchant. As well as its contemporary interiors reflecting the extravagant *fin-de-siècle* life-style of San Francisco's rich, the Society has a comprehensive collection of lithographs, watercolours, oil paintings and drawings relating to the history of San Francisco and California up to about 1906.
   The collection is presented in a regularly changing exhibition.

The Society's Library is situated just around the corner at 2099 Pacific Avenue. It has one of the most important collections of books, periodicals and photographs, etc. again relating to the history of the city and state. Open: Wed.– Sat. 10am–4pm.

★California Palace of the Legion of Honor (Museum)   B 9

No other museum outside France has so comprehensive a collection of French art as the California Palace of the Legion of Honor. Today it forms part of the museum's collection of European art from the Middle Ages to the early 20th c.

The Neo-Classical building, delightfully situated on a hill in Lincoln Park in the north-west of the city, is a copy of the Palais de la Légion d'Honneur in Paris. It was a gift from the German American Adolph B. Spreckels to his wife Alma, née Bretteville.

Although the original intention was that the California Palace of the Legion of Honor, opened in 1924, should be devoted exclusively to French art, in the course of time it became endowed with works by artists of other

Location
Lincoln Park

Buses
2, 38

Opening shortly after refurbishment

California Palace of the Legion of Honor

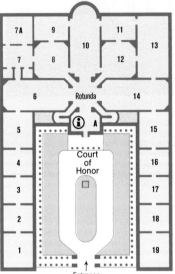

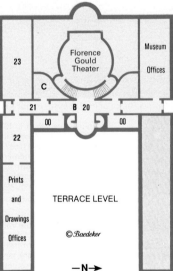

Rooms 1,2	Medieval art	
Room 3	German and Dutch Renaissance	
Room 4	14th and 15th c. Italian art	
Room 5	16th c. Italian, Spanish and French art; Titian, El Greco, etc.	
Room 6	17th and 18th c. Italian and French art	
Room 7	Robert Dollar Gallery: 18th c. French art	
Room 7A	Paris salon (18th c.)	
Room 8	D. and A. Wilsey Court: Rodin Sculpture	
Room 9	18th c. French applied art	

Room 10	Adolph B, and Alma Spreckels Rodin Gallery	
Room 11	Wattis Gallery: graphics (Achenbach Foundation)	
Room 12	W. and P. Shorenstein Court: sculptures by Rodin, Maillol, etc.	
Room 13	Temporary exhibitions	
Room 14	M. A. and H. Naify Gallery: 17th c. Dutch and Flemish masters (Rubens, Rembrandt, Hals, Van Dyck, etc.)	
Room 15	17th c. Dutch and Flemish painters (de Hooch, Steen, Ter Borch, Brueghal, etc.)	

Room 16	18th c. French art	
Room 17	19th c. Neo-Classical art	
Rooms 18,19	19th and early 20th c. (mainly French Impressionists; sculptures by Maillol, Degas, Rodin)	
Rooms 20–22	Graphics (Achenbach Foundation)	
Room 23	Porcelain	
A	Museum shop	
B	Telephone	
C	Café Chanticleer	
00	Toilets	
🛈	Information	

California Palace of the Legion of Honor – notable collection of French art

nationalities. When, in 1972, it was decreed, as a cost-saving measure, that the California Palace of the Legion of Honor should be combined with the de Young Museum (see Golden Gate Park) – both being the responsibility of the city – the non-French works were transferred to the de Young Museum which in turn handed over its French *objets d'art* to the California Palace. Since then both have undergone further reorganisation with European art now concentrated in the California Palace and US American art in the de Young Museum.

The museum has the munificence of three families – the Spreckels, the Huntingdons and the Williams – to thank for the greater part of its collection: Mr and Mrs Adolph Spreckels donated mainly 18th c. works, together with original bronze castings by Rodin. Mr and Mrs Archer B. Huntingdon bequeathed furniture, tapestries and a number of paintings. In 1944 Mr and Mrs H. K. S. Williams not only gave the museum a comprehensive collection of French art but also made available a large sum of money for the purchase of further works of art from France.

Collection

A detailed account of the collection is beyond the scope of this book although some idea of its range is conveyed by the accompanying floor plan of the museum.

Special mention should be made of an Angers tapestry made in 1380 and a complete 18th c. interior from the "Hôtel d'Humières" in Paris; also the paintings by Fra Angelico, Titian, El Greco, Tiepolo and Dutch masters such as Rubens, Hals, Van Dyke and Brueghel, and sculptures by Houdon, Canova and Rodin. In addition to these are works by major French painters such as Claude Lorrain, Nicolas Poussin, Georges de La Tour, François Boucher, Jean-Honoré Fragonard, Jean-Antoine Watteau, Louis David, Camille Corot, Gustave Courbet, Edgar Degas, Edouard Manet and Claude Monet.

The Achenbach Foundation for Graphic Arts is yet another attraction of the California Palace. It comprises a collection of graphic works amounting to more than 100,000 sheets dating from the 15th c. to the 20th c., and was presented to the city by Mr Moore Achenbach and his wife Sadie, whose wish was that it should be housed here.

Achenbach Foundation for Graphic Arts

Valuable illustrated books and a library of some 3000 volumes relating to the graphic arts form part of the collection.

★The Cannery (Shopping and leisure centre) H 7

Since 1967 an interesting complex with fashion houses, food shops, boutiques, art galleries, cafés and restaurants has been developed on the south side of Fisherman's Wharf (see entry), in what used to be the premises, now nearly a hundred years old, of the Del Monte fruit canning factory.

Location
2801 Leavenworth Street

Buses
15, 19, 30

There are similar developments at Ghirardelli Square and Pier 39 (see entries). Open-air concerts, poetry readings and other shows take place here.

Cable cars
59, 60

The Cannery is a fine example of the contribution being made by San Francisco's architects to urban renewal.

Opening times
Mon.–Sat.
10am–6pm, Sun.
11am–6pm; in
summer till 9pm
(restaurant till
midnight)

Musicians and entertainers perform in an inner courtyard where the olive trees are almost a hundred years old.

On the third floor Cannery Casuals boasts a notable Byzantine mosaic ceiling. From the Cannery there is also a splendid view of the harbour.

The Cannery – a centre for shopping and leisure

★Carmel

Location
106 miles/170km
south 118 miles/
190km via 17 Mile
Drive

Carmel (population 4800), delightfully situated on the Monterey Peninsula, was given its name by the Spanish seafarer Sebastian Vizcaino, in honour of three Carmelite monks who landed there with him in 1603, not far from the second Californian mission in Monterey (see entry). Settlement in Carmel proceeded slowly; at the beginning of the 20th c. it was still a small village with cows grazing in the fields. Then it was discovered by painters, writers and photographers and after the Second World War quickly became a mass tourist attraction. Today it is world famous, not least because in 1986 the film star Clint Eastwood was elected Mayor.

When to visit

Carmel enjoys mild weather throughout the year, 300 days of sunshine being the norm. Mornings, however, are often foggy in July (21 days), August (22 days) and September (16 days).

Tradition

The unending struggle between the champions of "progress" and preservation has happily resulted in compromise here, so that Carmel, its houses reminiscent of an English village, has scarcely changed and its charm has been retained. There are no street lamps, no neon advertising, few sidewalks and no house numbers (just signs saying "north of Ocean Avenue" or "west of San Carlos"). Monterey pines grow in the town centre. Mail is not delivered but collected from the post office on the south-east corner of 5th and Dolores Street. High heels are officially banned and eating in the street forbidden. There are no parking meters, multi-storey car parks or high-rise blocks. Street parking is restricted to an hour or two. The streets are patrolled by Carmel's force of 26 policemen and policewomen.

Tourism

Carmel has more than 50 restaurants (until recently no fast-food restaurants were allowed), some 70 galleries and 40 estate agents. The 1200 shops and firms providing services (in a community of fewer than 5000

Carmel: cottage-style houses . . .

. . . and statue of Fr. Junípero Serra

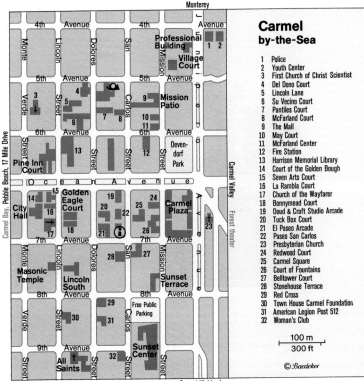

Carmel
by-the-Sea

1 Police
2 Youth Center
3 First Church of Christ Scientist
4 Del Dono Court
5 Lincoln Lane
6 Su Vecino Court
7 Pantiles Court
8 McFarland Court
9 The Mall
10 May Court
11 McFarland Center
12 Fire Station
13 Harrison Memorial Library
14 Court of the Golden Bough
15 Seven Arts Court
16 La Rambla Court
17 Church of the Wayfarer
18 Bonnymead Court
19 Doud & Craft Studio Arcade
20 Tuck Box Court
21 El Paseo Arcade
22 Paseo San Carlos
23 Presbyterian Church
24 Redwood Court
25 Carmel Square
26 Court of Fountains
27 Belltower Court
28 Stonehouse Terrace
29 Red Cross
30 Town House Carmel Foundation
31 American Legion Post 512
32 Woman's Club

100 m
300 ft

© Baedeker

people) are aimed at the masses of tourists who every year spend many millions of dollars here. In the peak season in particular the crush can be overwhelming – on weekdays about 500,000 cars drive through Carmel. Catering for mass tourism while preserving a cosy atmosphere is Carmel's secret. The majority of visitors confine themselves to the square mile of the town centre, only a few venturing into the residential areas or to the attractive little beach. Every year in the second half of July there is a Bach festival attracting big audiences. Quall Lodge (800 Valley Greens Drive) is one of the most luxurious hotels in California with a 270 acre/100ha park, lakes, meadows, woods, a large golf course, four tennis courts and two swimming pools.

Monterey Peninsula Visitors and Convention Bureau
Monterey, tel. 649–1770
Carmel Business Association, Carmel, tel. 624–2522.

Information

San Carlos Borromeo del Río Carmelo

Dating from 1770 Carmel's San Carlos Borromeo del Río Carmelo is the second oldest of the 21 missions founded in California by the Franciscans. Its architecture and location on Monterey Bay make the Carmel Mission, as

Location
3080 Río Road

45

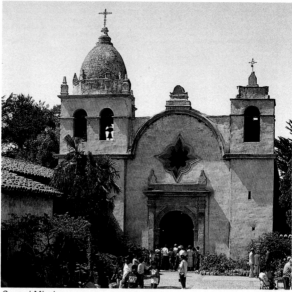

Carmel Mission

Opening times
Mon.–Sat.
9.30am–4.30pm
Sun.
10.30am–4.30pm

Tel. 805–624–3600

it is usually known, one of the most attractive. At the time of its building it represented the northernmost extent of Spanish rule. Father Junípero Serra, who founded the first nine Californian missions, from San Diego (1769) to San Buenaventura in Ventura (1782), died here in 1784 at the age of 71.

Restoration of the mission and its Moorish-style church, built in 1797 by a Mexican stone-mason, began in 1934. It is one of the few missions to have preserved its square inner court, where Serra's tomb is situated. Serra was beatified by Pope John Paul II on September 25th 1988 (despite protests from Indian groups who regard him as simply a Conquistador).

Inside the church there is a wooden figure of the Virgin which the missionary brought with him from Mexico. The spartanly furnished room with its wooden bed and desk from which Serra supervised the mission and the baptism of more than 5000 Indians, can also be seen.

Carmel Valley

When fog shrouds Carmel the Carmel Valley, just a few miles south-east (reached by Highway G 16 branching off the US 1), makes a delightful retreat. Situated on the Carmel River, the valley offers plentiful opportunity for outdoor activities such as fishing and swimming. It is also the location of the largest Zen Buddhist monastery in the United States.

★★Chinatown   I 8 (I/J 4/5)

Location
Grant Avenue
(main axis)
between
Columbus Avenue
and Bush Street

San Francisco has the largest Chinese population of any city outside Asia. The area along Grant Avenue between Bush Street and Columbus Avenue, together with the streets either side, is home to 100,000 Chinese. Chinatown is a city within the city, with Chinese shops, restaurants and distinctively Chinese institutions. English-speakers may still occasionally find themselves not understood – in restaurants for instance.

Chinatown Gateway, Bush Street

San Franciscan chinoiserie: street lamp . . .   *. . .and restaurant*

Chinatown

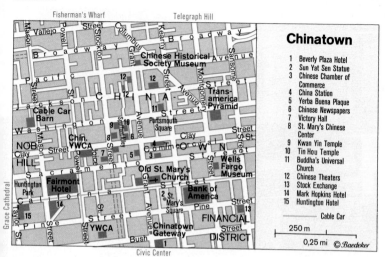

Fisherman's Wharf Telegraph Hill

Chinatown

1 Beverly Plaza Hotel
2 Sun Yat Sen Statue
3 Chinese Chamber of Commerce
4 China Station
5 Yerba Buena Plaque
6 Chinese Newspapers
7 Victory Hall
8 St. Mary's Chinese Center
9 Kwan Yin Temple
10 Tin Hou Temple
11 Buddha's Universal Church
12 Chinese Theaters
13 Stock Exchange
14 Mark Hopkins Hotel
15 Huntington Hotel

Cable Car

250 m

0,25 mi   © Baedeker

Civic Center

Guided tours
Ding How Tours
Tel. 981–8399

The Chinese began to settle in the area of Grant Avenue, or Calle del Fundación as the oldest street in San Francisco was then known, from 1850 onwards i.e. from just after the Gold Rush. Following its destruction in the 1906 earthquake, Chinatown was comprehensively rebuilt in Chinese style, ending up more attractive than it had been before the disaster. Now, with its temples, theatres, workshops, small businesses, stores, antique and souvenir shops, teahouses and pharmacies with their unfamiliar nostrums, the district has become one of the major sights of San Francisco.

The population of Chinatown has been expandingly rapidly in the last 30 years, due to an ever-increasing number of immigrants from Asia. More than ten per cent of San Franciscans are now of Chinese extraction. About one-fifth of the houses in Chinatown are Chinese-owned.

A walk around Chinatown

Chinatown Gateway

Any visit to Chinatown ought to start at Chinatown Gateway on the corner of Grant Avenue and Bush Street. Erected in 1970 the gate is of typical Oriental construction, decorated with dragons and other creatures. Like most San Francisco thoroughfares, Grant Avenue up to Bush Street was widened in the 19th c.; the part of the street running away beyond China-town Gate gives the best impression of what the city must once have looked like.

Old St Mary's Church

Old St Mary's Church (on the corner of Grant Avenue and California Street) is the oldest Catholic church in San Francisco. Built in 1854 it was badly damaged in the 1906 earthquake and also by a serious fire 60 years later. Having been restored its appearance today is very much as it was in San Francisco's early days. Originally a cathedral, it is now simply a parish church. The new St Mary's Cathedral (see entry) is situated in another part of town, on Cathedral Hill.

Carved above the clock dial is the admonition: "Son Observe the Time and Fly from Evil". In addition to the church the clergy house is also noteworthy. Designed by the New York architects Skidmore, Owings & Merrill, it was built in 1964.

From Old St Mary's Church there is a view of St Mary's Square. The site was presented to the city by the Catholic diocese in 1912. Beneath it today there is an underground garage. On the square stands Beniamino Bufano's statue of Dr Sun Yat-sen, the first president of the Republic of China (January 1st 1912–February 14th 1912). In the early part of the century he spent several years of political asylum in San Francisco.

St Mary's Square

A short distance north of Old St Mary's Church stands one of Chinatown's many Chinese-style telephone kiosks.

Telephone kiosk

The building belonging to the Soo Yuen Benevolent Institution on the corner of Grant Avenue and Clay Street was given its distinctive Chinese appearance only in 1912.

Soo Yuen Benevolent Association

San Francisco came into existence at the spot now occupied by Dick Young House (823 Grant Avenue), between Clay Street and Washington Street. It was here on June 25th 1835 that the first human habitation was erected in the new settlement of Yerba Buena, as San Francisco was originally called. It was actually a tent, replaced a few months later by the first timber houses.

Dick Young House

Tien How Temple is on the top floor of 125 Waverly Place (between Washington and Clay Streets). Originally founded in 1852 on a different site, the temple is dedicated to Tien How, the Buddhist Queen of Heaven. Non-Buddhists can visit the temple without too much difficulty (open: daily 9am–5pm, 7–9pm).

Tien How Temple

This building, erected relatively recently (1977) on the corner of Clay Street and Stockton Street, is the head office of the Kong Chow Benevolent Association, the oldest Chinese Friendly Society in America. Visiting times for the temple, which bears the same name, are displayed on the door.

Kong Chow Benevolent Association and Temple

Chinatown's central post office is on the third floor.

·Tin How Temple, named for the Buddhist Queen of Heaven

Chinatown

Chinese Six Companies

The headquarters of the Chinese Six Companies (843 Stockton Street) is perhaps the most important institution in Chinatown. In the 19th c. it recruited Chinese labourers, the so-called coolies (which roughly translated means "hard labour"), for construction work on the transcontinental railroad.

Later it acted as a sort of arbitrator, adjudicating in disputes among the Chinese. Although today it has lost something of its former prestige, it remains of considerable social significance.

Bank of Canton

The pagoda-like building on the corner of Grant Avenue and Washington Street is at present occupied by the Bank of Canton. It was built in 1909 as the Chinatown telephone office. From 1894 to 1949 there was a Chinese language telephone service which operated independently of the central San Francisco exchange; calls were put through manually. In 1847 the first San Francisco newspaper, the "California Star", was printed here.

Spofford Alley

Spofford Alley turns off between Clay Street and Washington Street. It is one of those intriguing alleyways of the sort found only in Chinatown. Beyond Washington Street it joins Old Chinatown Lane, once notorious for its numerous brothels and gambling halls.

Buddha's Universal Church

Buddha's Universal Church, at the corner of Washington Street and Kearny Street, was built in 1961 by members of the Pristine Orthodox Dharma, a strongly Americanised modern offshoot of Buddhism. It is the largest Buddhist temple in America.

On the roof of the temple are a lotus pool and Bodhi tree, the latter reputed to be a shoot from the tree beneath which Buddha achieved enlightenment (Bodhi) more than 2500 years ago. (Viewing by prior telephone arrangement only; tel. 982–6166.)

Bank of Canton: styled right for Chinatown

This museum, at 650 Commercial Street, is devoted to the history of the Chinese in America. Although the bulk of its exhibits, photographs and documents relate to the part played by the Chinese at the time of the California Gold Rush, the museum also has important material from later periods. Exhibits are labelled in both Chinese and English. The museum is open: Tue.–Sat. noon–4pm. It is closed on public holidays.

Chinese Historical Society of America Museum

Entry free

In and around John Street there are three Chinese theatres. The simplicity of staging, the music, unfamiliar to European ears, the marvellous costumes and the seemingly eventless plots of the plays performances of which would at one time last for days or even weeks, make for a thoroughly fascinating experience. Male actors traditionally took all the roles, including those of women.

Theatre

See Practical Information

Restaurants

Chinese Cultural Center

I 8 (J 4)

The Chinese Cultural Center came into existence when the Holiday Inn Hotel was completed and occupies the second floor of this building.

Location
750 Kearny St.

It is primarily a meeting place for San Francisco's Chinese community and incorporates a 650-seat auditorium in which cultural, political and religious events are held.

Opening times
Tue.–Sat.
10am–4pm

Closed
Public holidays

The Cultural Center also serves as a museum, displaying Chinese works of art and promoting other aspects of Chinese culture.

Entry free

City Hall

See Civic Center

★Civic Center

H 9 (H 6)

No other city in America has such a magnificent official and administrative centre as San Francisco. Its focal point is the square-shaped Civic Center Plaza around which are grouped various buildings – the huge City Hall, the Louise M. Davies Symphony Hall, the War Memorial Opera House and Veterans' Building, the Civic Auditorium, the Main Public Library, the Federal Building, the Federal Office Building, the State Office Building, etc.

Location
Market Street,
Van Ness Avenue,
McAllister Street

Buses
5, 31

Sat. 10am. Meet at the History Room of the Main Public Library.

Guided tours

City Hall

On the west side of the square stands the 300ft/92m-high City Hall, the fifth in San Francisco's history; its immediate predecessor, which stood on the site now occupied by the Main Public Library, collapsed prior to completion during the 1906 earthquake.

Opening times
During office
hours

The present building, constructed between 1912 and 1915, was designed by two Californian architects, John Bakewell and Arthur Brown jr., on the model of a French Renaissance château. It is nearly 400ft/120m long and 300ft/90m wide, with offices ranged around an interior courtyard beneath a

Guided tours
Thur. noon. Meet
at the History
Room of the Main
Public Library

City Hall in San Francisco's Civic Center

tall dome. At 300ft/90m it is even a few metres higher than the Capitol in Washington. The drum, encircled by pillars, reaches a height of 190ft/58m at which point the dome is 85ft/26m in diameter.

Inside the City Hall are the offices of the city's administration including the mayor's office, council chambers of the eleven-strong Board of Supervisors, and city courts. The building is an impressive manifestation of San Francisco's municipal pride. The City Hall work-force numbers some 1260 people.

Main Public Library

Information
Tel. 557–4000

The Main Public Library, headquarters of the city's library services, is on the east side of the square, opposite City Hall. The building was constructed in 1917 by George Kelham in Beaux-Arts style; the steel magnate Andrew Carnegie provided generous financial support. The library has a stock of some 1.2 million books, not to mention a considerable collection of newspapers and manuscripts (temporary exhibitions on the 2nd and 3rd floors). The building has long been too small to meet all the demands placed on it.

A city library was founded in San Francisco as long ago as 1879, at first occupying rented rooms in Bush Street. It began to loan out books in 1880. The present Main Public Library, which supports 26 branches throughout San Francisco, stands where, in 1906, the fourth City Hall collapsed in the earthquake while in process of completion. Earlier still it was the site of the Yerba Buena cemetery (before Yerba Buena was renamed San Francisco). Particularly noteworthy are two monumental murals by Frank DuMond in the reading and catalogue room; they depict scenes from California's pioneering days.

Behind the Main Public Library stands the Old Federal Building.

Main Public Library, built in 1917

Civic Auditorium (Conference Centre)

The Civic Auditorium, the oldest building in the Civic Center, occupies the south side of Civic Center Plaza. Together with its extension, Brooks Hall, constructed in 1958, the Auditorium serves the city as a conference centre. The Auditorium itself seats 8000 and was built in 1915 for the great Panama-Pacific Exhibition. The architect was Arthur Brown jr. who also designed the City Hall (with John Bakewell), the War Memorial Opera House and the Veterans' Building.

War Memorial Opera House

Like the Veterans' Building immediately north of it, the War Memorial Opera House, to the west of City Hall, was built in 1932 by Arthur Brown jr. Until 1980 the San Francisco Opera (founded in 1923) shared the Opera House with the San Francisco Symphony Orchestra, as a result of which their respective seasons could only be short. In 1980 the Symphony Orchestra moved to the newly built Louise M. Davies Symphony Hall.

The War Memorial Opera House and Veterans' Building were the venue for the Founding Assembly of the UN. The charter setting up the "World Parliament" was signed on the stage of the Opera House by the representatives of 43 nations on June 26th 1945. United Nations Plaza, a square at the east end of the Civic Center, commemorates this historic event.

★Louise M. Davies Symphony Hall

The opening of this concert hall in September 1980 was the fulfilment of a long-cherished ambition among San Francisco's music-lovers: it meant

Louise M. Davies Symphony Hall – San Francisco's ultra-modern concert hall

that at long last the Symphony Orchestra, which until then had shared the War Memorial Opera House with the San Francisco Opera and Ballet, had a home of its own.

The building, designed by New York architects Skidmore, Owings & Merrill in collaboration of Pietro Belluschi, was required to blend with the rest of the Civic Center while yet being modern in conception (there was no question of imitating the Art Deco style of the other buildings).

The result, both internally and externally, is a compromise between the old and new, tradition and modernity.

All in all it deserves its reputation as one of the most interesting new buildings in San Francisco. Though capable of seating 3000, it has an intimate feel to it. The acoustic problems which dogged it at the start have since been overcome so that San Francisco can today take justified pride in its concert hall financed entirely by private funds.

Coit Tower

See Telegraph Hill

Conservatory of Flowers

See Golden Gate Park

Victorian façades in Cow Hollow

Cow Hollow (District)   G 8

In the years following the Gold Rush the part of present-day Union Street west of Van Ness Avenue was a green valley. People used to call it "Cow Hollow" and the name has survived, though there have not been meadows or cows there for many a year. The area began to be developed about a century ago; in the last 25 years it has become a model of enlightened urban renewal. The numerous Victorian houses (see entry) have been beautifully restored, some being converted for commercial use.

Location
1600–2300
Union Street

Bus
41

Today there are fashion boutiques, antique shops, galleries and restaurants, as well as some of the city's best-known singles bars and cafés. Cow Hollow is a district which has rediscovered its style.

The side streets off Union Street between Octavia and Steiner Streets are also worth exploring; note in particular the houses at 2038 and 1980 Union Street, built in the 1870s by James Cudworth, a dairy-farmer. The house at 2038 is the largest former farmhouse remaining here.

Crocker Center

See Galleria at Crocker Center

De Young Memorial Museum

See Golden Gate Park

★Embarcadero Center

Location
between
Embarcadero,
Battery and Clay
Streets

MUNI station
(Embarcadero)

Buses
2, 7, 8, 21, 31,
42, 55, 71, 72

The Embarcadero Center complex fully deserves its reputation as one of the most interesting and original examples of urban renewal. The eight buildings – five skyscrapers of between 32 and 34 storeys, the 20-storey Hyatt Regency Hotel, the Park Hyatt San Francisco Hotel and the completely renovated Federal Reserve Bank – are the work of John Portman, an architect from Atlanta.

The first four skyscrapers, constructed between 1971 and 1982, are linked by pedestrian walkways providing access to more than 140 shops and restaurants. The fifth tower (Embarcadero Central West) was completed in 1988.

Because San Francisco's weather is so mild, people spend a lot of time in the open air. Particularly at midday considerable crowds gather in the plazas set on different levels between the buildings. Sculptures by a number of well-known artists adorn several of these open spaces.

Hyatt Regency
Hotel

Although the architecture of the skyscrapers is conventional, the Hyatt Regency Hotel, opened in 1973, never ceases to provoke comment. The N side, almost triangular in outline, inclines at an angle of 45 degrees; the rooms enjoy a fine view out over the Bay.

The hotel foyer is even more sensational: over 300ft/91m long it is 190ft/57m high, reaching up to the seventeenth storey. Around it are grouped the restaurant, bars and shops. The centre-piece of this unique space is a four storey-high sphere sculpted from gilded aluminium tubing by the American sculptor Charles Perry.

The Embarcadero Center, one of the most original examples of urban renewal

The vast foyer of the Hyatt Regency Hotel with its immense sculptured ball

The Exploratorium, Palace of Fine Arts

Exploratorium   F 7

Location
3601 Lyons Ave.,
near the Golden
Gate Bridge

Buses
22, 28, 30, 41,
43

This quite exceptional science museum is housed in the Palace of Fine Arts, the only survivor from among 323 large buildings constructed for the Panama-Pacific Exposition of 1915. The vast majority of the museum's 700 or so displays encourage visitor participation, which children particularly enjoy and which contributes greatly to the understanding of nature's workings.

The museum is open Tue.–Sun. 10am–5pm, Wed. until 9.30pm. Entry free on the first Wed. in the month.

Ferry Building   J 8 (K 4)

Location
Lower end of
Market Street

The Ferry Building, with its Neo-Romanesque façade and 230ft/70m-high tower modelled on the Giralda, the campanile of Seville Cathedral, is located at the lower end of Market Street (see entry), on the east side of Embarcadero Plaza. Erected by the state of California between 1896 and 1903, both the building and the tower survived the 1906 earthquake intact. The Ferry Building was once the symbol of San Francisco but has since lost this distinction to more recent additions, notably the Transamerica Pyramid (see entry).

Until the building of the San Francisco-Oakland and Golden Gate Bridges (see entries) all roads used to converge on the Ferry Building. Every day 170 ferries owned by various ferry companies maintained a shuttle service across the Bay. Nowadays these have been reduced to just a few ferries serving Sausalito (see entry), Larkspur and Tiburon (see entry).

California State
Division of
Mines Museum

As well as being the headquarters of the Port Authority, the Ferry Building houses the California State Division of Mines Museum incorporating a magnificent collection of rocks and minerals (open: Mon.–Fri 9am–5pm).

World Trade
Center

The World Trade Center, which has an exhibition of products from all parts of the globe, occupies the building's north wing (open: Mon.–Fri. 9am–3pm. Entry free).

★Fisherman's Wharf   H 7

Location
Jefferson Street

Buses
15, 19, 30, 32,
42

Cable cars
59, 60
(to terminus)

Fisherman's Wharf used to be not only a flourishing fishing harbour but also a real "Little Italy", the Genoese who made their homes here towards the end of the 19th c. having been joined in due course by Neapolitans, Calabrians and Sicilians. Even now this Italian influence is still in evidence.

Though the harbour itself has become somewhat run down, few of the 12 million tourists who come to San Francisco each year depart without visiting Fisherman's Wharf with its many shops, restaurants, waxworks and other such attractions. And there are still some fishermen, many of whom welcome paying tourists on their fishing trips (from the quay north of Jefferson Street between Jones Street and Leavenworth Street). Catches include crayfish and crabs, soles, salmon, etc. Most of the fish are destined for local restaurants.

Plans are afoot to redress the imbalance which has developed in recent decades between the traditional activities of the Wharf and the tourist-orientated trade, thus restoring to the area something of its original colour.

Fisherman's Wharf: seafood . . .   *. . . and juggler*

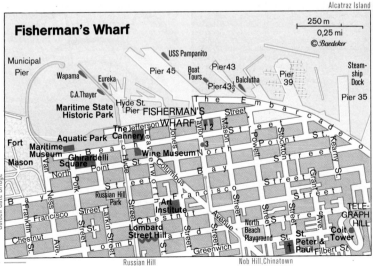

1 Ripley's "Believe It or Not" Museum   2 Wax Museum   3 St Francis Statue

Fisherman's Wharf

Small-craft harbour at Fisherman's Wharf

Fort Point

Galleria at Crocker Center

Fisherman's Wharf's little museums are very entertaining and well worth a visit.

The "Believe It or Not" Museum (175 Jefferson Street) has some 2000 curiosities from all corners of the globe (open: daily, 9 or 10am–11pm).

Further east at 145 Jefferson Street, the Wax Museum at Fisherman's Wharf (open: daily 10am–10pm) boasts 275 life-size wax figures of prominent people. The figures were brought over from England.

Museums

Fort Point
D 7

Fort Point lies below the Golden Gate Bridge (see entry) just a few minutes walk from Toll Plaza. It was built between 1853 and 1861 to protect San Francisco from attack but its 600-strong garrison and 120 cannon never fired a shot in anger, only in ceremonial salute.

Location
Golden Gate
National Recrea-
tion Area

The fort was evacuated in 1896. Between 1933 and 1937 it was used for site works during construction of the Golden Gate Bridge. In the Second World War about 100 soldiers were stationed there.

Buses
Golden Gate
Transit from
Market St. and
7th St. or No. 30
to Chestnut and
Fillmore, then
No. 28 to Toll
Plaza

In 1970 the US Congress declared Fort Point a National Historic Site, since when it has been gradually restored. As one of the earliest military buildings in the American West it is well worth a visit, especially if advantage is taken of one of the free daily guided tours. The fort is said to have been, in the 19th c., the largest brick structure west of the Mississippi.

Daily 10am–5pm. Closed Christmas Day and New Year's Day.

Opening times

Friends of Photography · Ansel Adams Center
I 9

This museum is the first in San Francisco to be devoted exclusively to photography and to the work of the celebrated Californian photographer Ansel Adams in particular.

Location
250 Forth Street,
south of Market
Street

One of the five galleries houses a permanent display of Adams' work and that of his successors. The other four are used for temporary exhibitions.

Opening times
Tue.–Sun.
11am–6pm

The museum, which was opened in 1991, has a library and a bookshop with a large selection of books on photography.

Galleria at Crocker Center
I 9

Situated on the corner of Post Street and Kearny Street, the 38-storey skyscraper known as the Crocker Center, designed by architects Skidmore, Owings & Merrill for the Crocker Bank, was built in 1983. With its pink granite façade it is widely considered one of the most pleasing of modern buildings.

Location
Corner of Post
Street/Kearny
Street

Information
Tel. 392–0100

Not least of the Crocker Center's attractions is the highly impressive Galleria, an arcade of elegant shops where daylight floods in.

The 50 or more shops and restaurants are open during normal hours Monday to Saturday. The roof garden, where lunchtime sandwiches or picnics can be consumed, is a welcome oasis in busy downtown San Francisco.

★Ghirardelli Square (Shopping and leisure centre) H 7

Location
900 North Front
Street

Buses
19, 30

Cable car
60

History of the
chocolate factory

Redevelopment

Belfry

Inaugurated in 1964 Ghirardelli Square was the first of a number of projects designed to breathe new life into abandoned factory complexes (others are The Cannery, Pier 39 and The Anchorage – see entries).

The old red brick building of the Ghirardelli chocolate factory has been transformed into the centre-piece of a shopping and leisure centre set amidst gardens with restful fountains and terraces with delightful views.

Domingo Ghirardelli was an Italian who arrived in newly founded San Francisco in 1849, the first year of the Gold Rush, via Uruguay and Peru. A trader in spices, coffee and cocoa, he later turned to chocolate-making.

The site occupied by Ghirardelli Square today, together with the woollen mill that stood on it, was acquired by his sons; the chocolate factory was built between 1900 and 1916. By the early 1960s it was standing empty, production having been transferred elsewhere.

The complex was then taken over by a group of San Francisco businessmen. They commissioned a number of different architects to design the centre with its more than 70 shops, galleries, cafés and cinema, arranged on three levels.

Today the development is thriving; Ghirardelli Square is a popular rendezvous for San Franciscans, particularly on warm evenings.

The belfry, dating from 1916, housed the chocolate factory's main offices. Its architect, William Mooser sen., took the Château de Blois in France as his model.

New lease of life for the old Ghirardelli chocolate factory

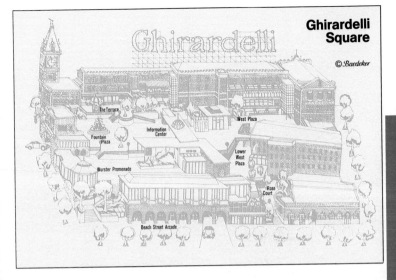

Ghirardelli Square

© Baedeker

The Terrace
West Plaza
Information Center
Fountain Plaza
Lower West Plaza
Wurster Promenade
Rose Court
Beach Street Arcade

The Ghirardelli Square gardens were laid out by Lawrence Halpin who also designed the concrete fountain in Rose Court. In East Plaza there is a particularly noteworthy bronze fountain by Ruth Asawa depicting two mermaids surrounded by turtles, water-lilies and dancing frogs.

Rose Court

★★Golden Gate Bridge

D 6/7

The Golden Gate Suspension Bridge connects San Francisco with Marin County and other districts further north. It was recently designated the greatest man-made sight in the United States by the US Travel Service. For years it was the symbol of San Francisco, though this distinction is now claimed by the Transamerica Pyramid. The splendid scenery all around makes it the most beautiful bridge in the world.

Buses
Golden Gate Transit from Market St. and 7th St. or No. 30 to Chestnut and Laguna then No. 28 to Toll Plaza

Opened on May 28th 1937, the bridge took four years to build, the director of the project being Joseph B. Strauss. Construction proved particularly difficult due to the strong cross-currents, and a number of fatal accidents occurred. At the time of its completion it was the longest suspension bridge in the world. On an average day it is used by more than 100,000 cars and lorries.

Toll
$3 (south-bound vehicles)
Pedestrians: no charge

The bridge, flood-lit in the evening, is approximately 2 miles/3km long and 90ft/27m wide. The carriageway is 220ft/67m above sea-level and the supporting towers 740ft/225m high.
   Every week 25 painters use about two tons of red lead ("International Orange") keeping the paintwork in good condition. Its striking colouring is one more reason why the Golden Gate Bridge is known throughout the world.

Of the many places from which good views of the bridge can be obtained, Coit Tower on Telegraph Hill (see entry) is perhaps the best. But this marvel of civil engineering should also be inspected from close range. Before

Views of the bridge

San Francisco's Golden Gate with the city and bay beyond

crossing on foot bear in mind that there is almost always a cool breeze blowing in off the Pacific even when the sun is out, so take warm clothes. They will also be needed if a mist suddenly comes down. Safety measures on the bridge include a wire-netting screen intended to deter anyone contemplating suicide – there have already been 900 – from throwing themselves into the water.

A monument to its builder, Joseph B. Strauss, stands at the end of the bridge. Strauss constructed more than 400 major steel bridges all over the world, including one in St Petersburg.

Keen walkers have the option to proceed on foot all the way from Hyde Street (terminus of cable car 60) via Golden Gate Promenade to the bridge. The distance is over 3 miles/5km but it makes an interesting walk.

1987 Jubilee

On May 24th 1987, its 50th anniversary, the Golden Gate Bridge was shut to motor traffic while cyclists and pedestrians enjoyed unfettered access. It is estimated that 250,000 people took advantage of the occasion to assemble on the bridge. In the evening the structure was illuminated throughout its length for the very first time.

Golden Gate National Recreation Area   D 7–A 1

Information
Fort Mason,
entrance Bay St.
and Franklin St.

Buses
30 to Chestnut
and Laguna

In 1972 the US Congress decreed the creation of a large leisure park in San Francisco and Marin County on the other side of the Bay, partly to prevent the coastal area from becoming built up or blighted by industry.

The park, covering an area of some 600sq.miles/1600sq.km, was christened the Golden Gate National Recreational Area. Every weekend many thousands of San Franciscans take advantage of its wide open spaces. There are islands, stretches of seashore, small-craft harbours, buildings of

historic interest and, in the Marin County section, wildlife reserves, picnic places and over 90 miles/150km of footpaths.

★★Golden Gate Park

B–E 10

Golden Gate Park is 3miles/5km long, ½ mile/800m wide and occupies 1017 acres/4.1sq.km. It is San Francisco's "lungs", the city itself having only one or two small parks. Before development began in 1871 this was an area of arid dunes, and it was only with the greatest difficulty that what was then the largest man-made park in the world was brought to its present appearance. The credit for this lies chiefly with one man, John McLaren, Park Commissioner for 56 years from 1887 to 1943.

Nowadays visitors to the park enjoy a grand network of footpaths and cycle tracks, more than 5000 different kinds of plants and dozens of species of trees, several lakes, bridle-paths, a buffalo paddock, three museums, a Japanese tea garden, greenhouses, a botanical garden and considerably more besides. The accompanying sketch-plan shows the general layout.

Strolling through Golden Gate Park is a delight, but very time consuming. Bear in mind also that after 3pm when the mist tends to come rolling in from the Pacific, the park can suddenly seem a less welcoming place.

Location
between Fulton St., Stanyan St., Lincoln Boulevard. and the Great Highway

Buses
5 and 21 (N side, museums),
7 (E side, greenhouses) 71 and 72 (S side, Strybing Arboretum)

★California Academy of Sciences (Museum)

The California Academy of Sciences stands in the eastern end of Golden Gate Park. It is the most important scientific institution in the state. Created

Location
Golden Gate Park

Golden Gate Park

Entrance court of the California Academy of Sciences in Golden Gate Park

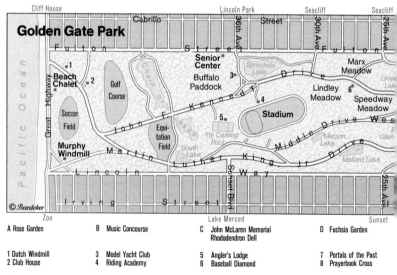

A Rose Garden	B Music Concourse	C John McLaren Memorial Rhododendron Dell	D Fuchsia Garden

1 Dutch Windmill	3 Model Yacht Club	5 Angler's Lodge	7 Portals of the Past
2 Club House	4 Riding Academy	6 Baseball Diamond	8 Prayerbook Cross

in 1853, only four years after the founding of San Francisco, it attracts a million and a half visitors a year.

The collections are mainly devoted to natural history: in the west wing minerals, fossils, mammals and North American birds; in the east wing an African section and rooms dedicated to anthropology, botany and space.

Opening times
daily 10am–5pm
(7pm in summer)

The Steinhart Aquarium, at the end of the court with the great fountain, has a collection of more than 14,000 aquatic creatures and is one of the biggest of its type in the world. 10,000 fish, dolphins, reptiles (e.g. alligators) and other species inhabit the aquarium's 250 tanks.

Steinhart
Aquarium

The Morrison Planetarium houses the first "Theater of the Stars" made in the United States (in 1951–52) rather than imported from Germany. 3800 star patterns are projected on to a dome 65ft/20m in diameter. The programme is revised annually.

Morrison
Planetarium

The Laserium is one of the park's more unusual attractions. Concerts with laser lights are presented daily.

Laserium

The Wattis Hall of Man has life-size displays illustrating the evolution of Man. Other rooms focus on animals, plants, minerals and precious stones.

Wattis Hall
of Man

Entry to any part of the California Academy of Sciences is free on the first Wednesday of the month. Otherwise an entrance fee is charged with additional fees for the Planetarium and the Laserium.

Entry

★M. H. de Young Memorial Museum

The M. H. de Young Memorial Museum is the oldest museum in San Francisco. While art and period interiors from North America – especially the USA from the Colonial period to the 20th c. – feature strongly in the

Bus
5 (to Fulton Street
and 8th Avenue)

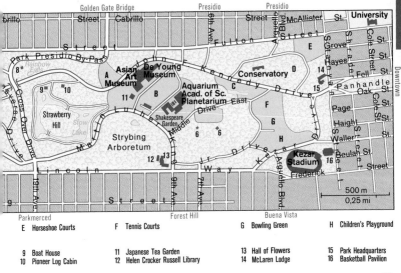

E	Horseshoe Courts	F	Tennis Courts	G	Bowling Green	H	Children's Playground
9	Boat House	11	Japanese Tea Garden	13	Hall of Flowers	15	Park Headquarters
10	Pioneer Log Cabin	12	Helen Crocker Russell Library	14	McLaren Lodge	16	Basketball Pavilion

Golden Gate Park

M.H.de Young Memorial Museum

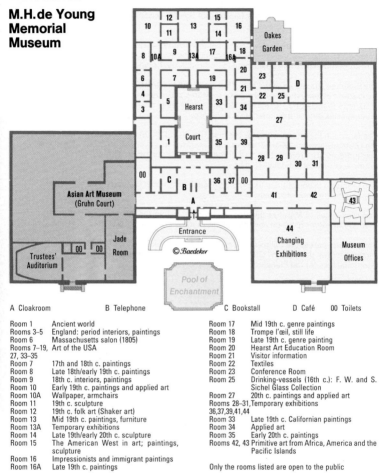

A Cloakroom   B Telephone   C Bookstall   D Café   00 Toilets

Room 1	Ancient world	Room 17	Mid 19th c. genre paintings
Rooms 3–5	England: period interiors, paintings	Room 18	Trompe l'œil, still life
Room 6	Massachusetts salon (1805)	Room 19	Late 19th c. genre painting
Rooms 7–19,	Art of the USA	Room 20	Hearst Art Education Room
27, 33–35		Room 21	Visitor information
Room 7	17th and 18th c. paintings	Room 22	Textiles
Room 8	Late 18th/early 19th c. paintings	Room 23	Conference Room
Room 9	18th c. interiors, paintings	Room 25	Drinking-vessels (16th c.): F. W. and S.
Room 10	Early 19th c. paintings and applied art		Sichel Glass Collection
Room 10A	Wallpaper, armchairs	Room 27	20th c. paintings and applied art
Room 11	19th c. sculpture	Rooms 28–31,	Temporary exhibitions
Room 12	19th c. folk art (Shaker art)	36,37,39,41,44	
Room 13	Mid 19th c. paintings, furniture	Room 33	Late 19th c. Californian paintings
Room 13A	Temporary exhibitions	Room 34	Applied art
Room 14	Late 19th/early 20th c. sculpture	Room 35	Early 20th c. paintings
Room 15	The American West in art; paintings, sculpture	Rooms 42, 43	Primitive art from Africa, America and the Pacific Islands
Room 16	Impressionists and immigrant paintings		
Room 16A	Late 19th c. paintings	Only the rooms listed are open to the public	

Opening times
Wed.–Sun.
10am–5pm

Entrance fee
1st Wed. of
month (all day)
and 1st Sat.
10am–noon
entry free

collection, there are also many exhibits from Egypt, Greece, Rome and the Near East. British art, and folk art from Africa, America and the Pacific Islands, are also represented.

The original museum building was an art gallery, purpose-built for the International Californian Exposition held in Golden Gate Park in 1894. Afterwards the Exposition's director, the newspaper proprietor Michael H. de Young (1849–1925), was charged with setting up a permanent museum. The collection at that time consisted of just a few items remaining from the exhibition. Over the next quarter of a century benefactions made possible the continuous, planned expansion of the museum, as a result of which more and more extensions were added until, in 1921, the old building in Egyptian style – of which two sphinxes are the only remaining sign – was finally replaced by more up-to-date premises.

North American Indian art in the M. H. de Young Memorial Museum

It was at this time that the museum was given its present name, acknowledging the contribution of its founder and earliest benefactor. Today it has some 40 galleries and more than 200,000sq.ft/18,500sq.m of exhibition space. The inner court is named after the newspaper magnate William Randolph Hearst (see Famous People), proprietor of the "San Francisco Examiner", who was determined not to be outdone by his colleague M. H. de Young, proprietor of the "San Francisco Chronicle", when it came to endowing the museum.

Unlike the majority of American museums this one is not privately run; it depends entirely for its support on the city which, a few years ago, found itself obliged to charge for admission. The ticket includes same-day admission to the adjoining Asian Art Museum of San Francisco (see below) and the California Palace of the Legion of Honor (see entry).

The museum's collection of North American paintings, sculptures and furnishings from the mid 17th to the mid 20th c. is particularly fine, due in large measure to John D. Rockefeller's gift of a comprehensive collection of American art including 175 paintings. Among the items on display is the oldest work of art in the museum and probably the oldest picture to have been painted in North America. It is by an anonymous Massachusetts artist and dates from about 1670.

North American art

18th and 19th c. American painting is represented by, among others, John Singleton Copley, Charles Tilson Peale, Benjamin West, John Trumbull, Thomas Cole and Caleb Bingham.

American painters

Of the various period interiors (furniture, carpets, silverware, applied art, etc.), a Massachusetts salon dating from 1805 and an English dining-room in the elegant Neo-Classical style created by the Scottish architect Robert Adam (1728–92), deserve special mention.

Period rooms

Primitive art

Rooms 42 and 43 feature primitive art from Africa, America and the Pacific Islands.

★Asian Art Museum of San Francisco

Bus
5 (to Fulton Street and 8th Avenue)

Opening times
daily 10am–5pm
(library: Wed.–
Sun. 10am–5pm)
1st Wed. of month
10am–8.45pm

Closed
Public holidays

Entrance fee
Free on 1st Wed.
of month

The Asian Art Museum of San Francisco, opened in 1966 and occupying the west wing of the M. H. de Young Memorial Museum, is one of the most unusual museums in America. What makes it remarkable – only the Hirshhorn Museum in Washington compares in this respect – is that 95% of its acquisitions derive from the collection of one man, in this case Avery Brundage.

Brundage, a wealthy businessman perhaps best known as a long serving President of the International Olympic Committee, began to take an interest in oriental art in 1936. He built up a private collection which, in 1959, he offered to the city of San Francisco "to bridge the gap between East and West". It was decided to build a special museum, which was not completed until 1966. From the outside the building is somewhat undistinguished.

During the intervening seven years Brundage had continued to build up his collection; he presented these new acquisitions to San Francisco as well. Then, on his death in 1975 at the age of 88, the museum also received the rest of his collection of works of art in the form of a legacy. As a result there are now nearly 10,000 sculptures, paintings, bronzes, ceramics, jade carvings and architectural fragments from Japan, Korea, China, India, Iran and other Asiatic cultures.

The hope is that, over the years, the museum can become one of the Western World's major centres for Asiatic art and culture. Its collections and publications to date lend every support to these hopes. It is unquestionably one of the most important museums in San Francisco, with something to offer every visitor, not just specialists in Asiatic art.

Khmer sculptures in the Asian Art Museum

Almost half the Brundage collection consists of items of Chinese origin. They occupy the entire ground floor; the Jade Room alone is worth the admission price. The upper floor houses works of art from other Asian countries – Iran, Turkey, Syria, Afghanistan, India, Pakistan, Mongolia, Korea, Japan and Indonesia.

The frequent special exhibitions of Asiatic art loaned by private collectors and other museums mean that barely 10% of the permanent collection can be displayed. To overcome this difficulty exhibits are rotated from time to time.

As a result it is not possible to pick out individual items for description here. Those on show at any given time are arranged chronologically.

While the examples of Chinese lacquerwork and ebony carving are exceptional, Brundage collected relatively few Chinese paintings. This left some gaps to be filled, which a generous acquisitions fund has fortunately made possible. The museum now possesses more than 150 Chinese rolls and bark paintings, though only a few are at present on show.

Chinese
Department

The museum's chief attraction is the Jade Room. With about 1200 jade works of art it is the largest collection in any Western country. Virtually all Chinese periods are represented from the 5th c. B.C. onward, though the emphasis is mainly on the Ming and Ch'ing periods (c. A.D. 1400–1900).

Jade Room

Although relatively small, the Japanese Department contains fine pieces from almost every period.
  Brundage became interested in collecting the art of India, Indonesia and Indochina only in his later years, as a consequence of which these departments are inferior in both quantity and quality to the collections of Chinese art.

Other
departments

The library, with 12,000 volumes on the art of the Near and Far East, is open to visitors as well as specialists. Students and museum staff from the USA, Japan, Taiwan and Korea come here for specialist training in Asiatic art.

Library

★Japanese Tea Garden (Zen Garden)

A further attraction of the Golden Gate Park and one of the real sights of the city is the Japanese Tea Garden. Like the M. H. de Young Memorial Museum it dates back to the 1894 California International Exposition. At the time it was the setting for a Japanese village of which it was a part. Now it forms a delightful adjunct to the Asian Art Museum adjacent to it.

Opening times
8am–to dusk

The layout of the garden was entrusted to a Japanese, Makoto Hagiwara, who looked after it for the next three decades, living on the site. His work was then carried on by his daughter, son-in-law and grandson.

During the Second World War the Hagiwaras, like many other Japanese, were interned; the Japanese Tea Garden became the Oriental Tea Garden and several of its houses were demolished. One was converted into a souvenir shop. It was not until 1952 that the garden had its original name restored.

The following year a lantern of peace was hung up and the Zen Garden was laid out, gifts from the children of Japan to the American people. Since then its Japanese-Buddhist character has been ever more strongly emphasised. The gaily coloured pagoda and the moon bridge are special attractions. The garden is a particularly lovely sight in spring when many cherry trees are in bloom and the cherry blossom festival is celebrated in Japantown (see entry).

Impression of the Japanese Tea-Garden in Golden Gate Park

Bird's-eye view of the Conservatory of Flowers

Strybing Arboretum (Botanic garden)

Opposite the Japanese Tea Garden, on the other side of Martin Luther King jr. Drive, lies the 26 acre/10ha Strybing Arboretum, named after Helen Strybing who endowed it.

The Arboretum contains more than 5000 clearly labelled species of plant grouped according to their region of origin. There are also ducks and swans to be seen which visitors may feed. Peacocks with their decorative tails add colour to the lawns and gravelled paths.

A plan available at the entrance illustrates the overall layout. There are also excellent guided tours (daily 10.30am and 1.30pm; from the kiosk) which take in all the beauties of this very special feature of Golden Gate Park.

Conservatory of Flowers

The Conservatory of Flowers is the oldest building in Golden Gate Park and probably the best example of Victorian architecture in the San Francisco area. Purchased in England, it was shipped to San Francisco via Cape Horn and re-erected here in 1879. It is now a protected building.
  In the conservatory, as well as a tropical garden, orchids, ferns and other foliage plants, there are displays of various varieties of flowers – arum lilies, begonias, chrysanthemums and many others according to season.

Grace Cathedral H 8 (I 4)

This Neo-Gothic church, clearly influenced in its architecture by Notre Dame in Paris, was dedicated in 1964, having taken 36 years to build. It

Grace Cathedral

Buses
71, 72 (to 9th Avenue & Lincoln Way)

Opening times
Mon.–Fri.
8am–4.30pm
Sat., Sun. and public holidays
10am–5pm

Bus
7 (to terminus)

Opening times
daily
8am–4.20pm

Location
1051 Taylor Street

Grace Cathedral on Nob Hill – it took 36 years to build and was completed in 1964

73

Cable car
61 (California
Street)

replaced an earlier church which stood lower down Nob Hill and which was destroyed in the 1906 earthquake. Grace Cathedral is the seat of the Episcopalian Bishop of California.

Although overall the church is modelled on Notre Dame, Florentine art inspired the main portals. These take the form of casts from Lorenzo Ghiberti's "Gates of Paradise" adorning the Baptistery in Florence.

Interior

The interior houses a number of notable works of art including a 13th c. Catalonian crucifix, a Flemish altarpiece dating from the late 15th c., a silk and gold Brussels Gobelin tapestry from the 16th c., a terracotta relief of the Madonna and Child by the Renaissance artist Antonio Rossellino and, on the north wall of the ambulatory, a collection of pages from medieval bibles illustrating the history of bible reproduction.

Also of particular interest are stained glass windows from the workshops of Charles Connick, Henry Lee Willet, Mark Adams and Gabriel Loire. The great east rose-window (by Loire, 1963) is illuminated after dark from within the building. The Cathedral has a celebrated choir of men and boys; recitals are often given on the Cathedral organ which has 7286 pipes. The 44 bells in the north tower are rung every evening; the hour bell, weighing six tonnes, is the largest in the West.

Haas-Lilienthal House

G 8 (G/H 4)

Location
2007 Franklin
Street

Haas-Lilienthal House is one of the largest private residences in San Francisco. It has remained quite unspoilt for nearly a century, with just one or two additions made. Designed by the architect Peter R. Schmidt, it was

Haas-Lilienthal House – a private residence in the Eastlake style

constructed in 1886 for William Haas, a wholesale grocer who had emigrated from Bavaria. The so-called Eastlake style was chosen, with a Queen Anne tower. The asymmetrical placing of cubes, cones, pyramids, cylinders and other geometrical forms is the most striking feature.

Most unusually for the time, the house was fully wired for electricity, though candle sconces were provided in the candelabra just in case. Including everything, down to the very last cent, the builder's bill is said to have amounted to only $18,500.

Until the end of the 1970s the house was still lived in by descendants of the original owner. Since then it has been the offices of the Foundation for San Francisco's Architectural Heritage which works to preserve the best of the city's architecture. The Ball Room is still used for its original purpose; it is hired out for various social functions.

Bus
2

Opening times
Wed. noon–4pm
Sun. 11am–4.30pm

Hyde Street Pier

See National Maritime Museum

Jackson Square

I 8 (J/K 4)

Historically speaking Jackson Square is one of the most interesting parts of San Francisco. Contrary to the expectations aroused by its name, it is not actually a square. It consists of Block 400 on Jackson Street and neighbouring side streets where a number of 19th c. business premises have been preserved. Most have been given a new lease of life as show rooms for interior designers, but there are also several other equally interesting shops.

Location
Bounded by Pacific, Montgomery, Washington, and Battery Streets

Jackson Square was the first part of San Francisco to be designated an area of historic interest (in 1972). Most of the buildings are now protected, among them:

No. 407: the warehouse of the Ghirardelli Chocolate Factory; built in 1860 and in use until 1894.

Nos. 415–31: the Ghirardelli Chocolate Factory; built in 1853 and in use until 1894.

No. 432: incorporating parts of the old Tremont Hotel, built in 1855 and later demolished.

No. 441: erected in 1861 over the buried wreckage of two ships abandoned during the Gold Rush.

No. 470: dating from 1852 this house was successively the Spanish, Chilean and French Consulates. It was also at one time the editorial offices of "La Parola", an Italian-language newspaper.

No. 472: one of the oldest (1850–52) and, in its simplicity, most handsome office buildings of its period in San Francisco; French Consulate from 1865 to 1875.

Nos. 445, 463–73 and 451: the first group date from 1860, the latter from 1866. They were built by Anson Parsons Hotaling, a well-known liquor-dealer of the time.

Most of these buildings survived the 1906 earthquake unscathed; a few suffered slight damage and were repaired.

The former tobacco warehouse around the corner at 722–28 Montgomery Street was converted in 1958 into law offices by the noted defence attorney and damages specialist Melvin Belli.

Japanese Tea Garden

See Golden Gate Park

Japantown

Location
bounded by Post
Street, Geary,
Laguna, and
Fillmore Streets

Buses
1, 2, 3 and 38
(to Laguna St.)

San Francisco's Japantown district is the cultural and business centre for the city's Japanese community, the first of whom arrived in San Francisco, the city they called Soko, over 120 years ago. It was only after the 1906 earthquake, however, that they started to settle in this particular area, Japantown or Nihonmachi as it is known in Japanese.

During the Second World War most of San Francisco's Japanese and Japanese-Americans ("Nisei") were interned. On their release many of the former went back to Japan; the others gradually returned to pick up the threads of their lives in the district they had left. Today there are more than 12,000 Japanese resident in San Francisco.

The opening of the Japan Center in 1968 was a great boost to the district. Now there are Japanese hotels, numerous Japanese and Korean restaurants, about 40 shops and a theatre. In addition to the Japanese Peace Pagoda, the principal sight of the district, the temple, shrines, art exhibitions and many shops make for a visit filled with interest.

The springtime Sakura Matsuri (Cherry Blossom Festival; see Practical Information, Events) is held in Peace Plaza with its five-storeyed Peace Pagoda. Entry is via a gate ("romon") designed by Yoshiro Taniguchi.

Justin Herman Plaza and the Ferry Building tower

Justin Herman Plaza   I 8 (K 4)

This small park in front of the Hyatt Regency Hotel was created in the course of developing the Embarcadero Center (see entry). It is popular with office workers from the nearby skyscrapers, who gather here during the midday break to eat their lunches and be entertained by assorted musicians and street actors.

Location
Where Market St. begins, opposite the Ferry Building

A notable feature of the park is the Vaillancourt Fountain, constructed by the Canadian sculptor Armand Vaillancourt out of colossal concrete blocks on which it is possible to clamber.

★Lombard Street   H 7 (H 3)

A short section of this street on Russian Hill has become one of the city's chief sights.

Cable car
60 (to the corner of Hyde Street & Lombard Street)

Extending the length of just a single block it has been nicknamed "the crookedest street in the world", having a fall of 14% negotiated by ten zigzag bends. This "crooked" section is planted out with hydrangeas, giving it a delightful appearance.

Few visitors with cars can resist this major attraction. Most people drive east up Lombard Street from the Pacific side to the junction with Hyde Street, then descend through the crooked section before continuing to Columbus Avenue. Steps in the sidewalk make the descent easy for those on foot.

Challenge for drivers: Lombard Street – the "crookedest street in the world"

Louise M. Davies Symphony Hall

See Civic Center

Maiden Lane   I 9 (I/J 5)

Location
East side of
Union Square,
between Post and
Geary Streets

Maiden Lane, once notorious for its pot-houses and brothels, is now one of the smartest shopping streets in San Francisco with exclusive shops selling high-quality goods.

One of the houses in the street, No. 140, is of particular architectural interest, being the only building in San Francisco designed by the famous architect Frank Lloyd Wright. With its distinctive internal ramp the house is, in the opinion of many, an early sketch for Wright's Guggenheim Museum building in New York. This oft expressed idea is, however, mistaken.

Although 140 Maiden Lane was completed in 1953, four years before work on the Guggenheim started, Wright's plans for the museum were put forward even earlier, in the late 1940s.

Today the house is an art gallery.

Main Public Library

See Civic Center

View of Market Street and the business district

Market Street   I 8–F 12 (K 4–H 6)

Impressive Market Street, one of the few thoroughfares to cut diagonally across the grid-iron pattern of San Francisco's streets, forms the boundary between the poorer south of the city and the more well-to-do north.

    This division has its origin in the urban plan drawn up in 1847 by the engineer Jasper O'Farrell at the behest of the military authorities. O'Farrell proposed two distinct networks of streets, one of relatively narrow streets and smaller blocks to the north, the other with wider streets (15ft/5m wider than in the north) and correspondingly larger blocks to be built on what was then marshland to the south.

    Market Street, separating them, was planned as a boulevard almost 130ft/40m wide. Because the two networks do not coincide, getting from a point south of Market Street to a destination north of it, or vice versa, can be quite tricky even today. Streets on both sides are numbered starting from Market Street and those that cross Market Street undergo a change of direction. It is a standing joke among San Franciscans that "no street has so many crossings and so little hope of getting across".

Urban plan

Of the districts on either side of Market Street it was those to the south with the wider streets which fell upon the hardest times. To reverse this trend and prevent the spread of urban blight to northern districts, the complete redevelopment of Market Street was decided upon. Between 1964 and 1979 more than $50m was ploughed into its revitalisation, in the process of which the street has been transformed, at least from the Ferry Building (see entry) to Powell Street. Trees have been planted, the sidewalks repaved in red stone, bus shelters erected and the whole appearance altered by the construction of numerous skyscrapers. Beyond Powell Street the development plan, brainchild of the architect John Carl Warnecke, has yet to achieve the desired results.

Redevelopment

At the south-west end of Market Street lies Twin Peaks, at the north-east end Embarcadero Plaza and the Ferry Building (see entries) on San Francisco Bay. Where Powell Street leaves Market Street, on the left is the southern cable car turntable (see Cable Cars). Behind it rise the 46-storey San Francisco Hilton, completed in 1971, with a viewing platform 492ft/150m up, and the Parc Fifty Five Hotel, opened in 1984.

Surroundings

North beyond the cable car turntable stands the Westin St Francis Hotel built in 1904. Its 335ft/120m-high tower with a panoramic bar at the top was added in 1972. Union Square (see entry) is off to the right.

Mexican Museum   G 7

The Mexican Museum is the only museum in the United States devoted entirely to Mexican art and folk culture from the pre-Columbian period to the present day. It is particularly rich in ceramics. Other interesting exhibits include paintings by chicanos, the Mexican farm-hands who come to the United States to help with the harvest. Open: Wed.–Sun. noon–5pm, 1st Wed. of month noon–8pm, entry free.

    On the second Saturday of every month the museum arranges a guided tour, departing 10am, of the many fascinating murals to be seen in Mission District. Many of the murals show the strong influence of Mexican artists such as Rivera and Orozco.

Location
Fort Mason,
Building D

Bus
30

M. H. de Young Memorial Museum

Golden Gate Park

★Mission Dolores G 11

Location
Dolores Street
and 16th Street

MUNI station
16th Street

Opening times
daily 9am–4pm

Closed
Thanksgiving Day,
Christmas Day,
New Year's Day

Entrance fee

Mission Dolores, or, to give it its proper title, the Mission San Francisco de Assisi, was the sixth of 21 missions founded on the California coast by Franciscans from Mexico. Father Junípero Serra (b. 1713 in Petrá, Majorca, d. 1784 in Carmel – see entry) laid the foundation-stone on October 9th 1776. The building, completed in 1791, is thus the oldest in San Francisco. It is 110ft/34m long and 21ft/6m wide with walls nearly 4ft/1.2m thick. The restored ceiling is decorated with pictures painted by Indians using pigments made from natural dyes. In the mission there were a total of 28,000 baptisms, mainly of Indians.

The basilica close by the mission dates from 1918; an earlier church was, unlike the mission, destroyed in the 1906 earthquake. The Baroque altar comes from Mexico. Documents about the history of the mission are displayed in a special room. The cemetery, later reduced in size, was used for burials from the 1780s until the end of the 19th c. Among those laid to rest were more than 5000 Indians who perished in the two great measles epidemics of 1814 and 1826.

As well as being one of the few sights in San Francisco south of Market Street (see entry), Mission Dolores is also the only one of the 21 missions to be now in the centre of a great city and thus easily visited.

★Monterey

Location
99miles/160km S of
San Francisco
(Coastal Highway
1 or Highway 101)

Monterey, which today has a population of 29,000, is beautifully situated on Monterey Bay; it also has an interesting history. From 1770 to 1822 it was the capital of Spanish California, at a time when Los Angeles, San Francisco and the present-day capital Sacramento had not even been founded. After Mexico declared its independence from Spain, Monterey continued in the role of provincial capital for another 24 years; but soon afterwards its political importance began to wane.

The town's fish canning industry collapsed decades ago when the sardine disappeared from the waters around Monterey; it has been left a notable literary memorial in the form of John Steinbeck's novel "Cannery Row". Today tourism is the economic mainstay. There are numerous good hotels, motels and restaurants, a complete list of which can be obtained from the Chamber of Commerce, 380 Alvarado Street, tel. 408–649–3200.

When to visit

The best time to visit the peninsula is in the period September to June, the three summer months being often marred by fog and low cloud. Rain can be expected in January and February.

Cannery Row

The major attraction in Monterey is obviously Cannery Row. Today the factories have been converted into a complex of restaurants, shops, galleries and a superb aquarium (see below); all that remains of the world of Steinbeck's novel are the walls of the buildings themselves.

No. 851

Kalisa's Lak Ida Café, built in 1929; from 1936 it was a brothel (immortalised by Steinbeck) and now, since the mid fifties, a coffee house.

No. 835

Opened in 1918 as the Chinese Wing Chong Grocery (Steinbeck's "Cannery Row" starts with a description of the shop, Won Yee from the top floor appearing as Lee Chong); now has some Steinbeck memorabilia.

No. 800

Pacific Biological Laboratory, called the Western Biological Laboratory by Steinbeck, where he passed many an hour in the years between 1930 and 1935.

Mission Dolores

The site of Flora Wood's "Lone Star Café" (Steinbeck's Dora Flood's "Lone Star Café/Bear Flag Restaurant"), from 1923 to 1941 another brothel; the present concrete building is an antique shop.

No. 799

Formerly the Monterey Canning Co. warehouse; now converted into shops and a fish restaurant.

No. 711

The second of Monterey's "Little Chinas" where Mr Wu and Mr Sam had their hotels; the present elegant Spindrift Inn was built some years ago.

Nos. 650, 654

Once the site of a grand villa destroyed by fire in 1924, and later of a fish canning factory; now the luxury Monterey Plaza Hotel.

No. 400

Former site of the Enterprise Cannery; now replaced by another luxury hotel, the Monterey Bay Inn.

No. 242

The Monterey State Historic Park includes several interesting old houses. Most are on the "Path of History" (marked by a red sign) and open daily 10am–6pm unless noted otherwise below.

Monterey State Historic Park

Corner of Scott and Oliver Street (open: Wed.–Sun. only): a restored grocer's shop dating from 1845.

Casa del Oro

Corner of Pacific and Del Monte Street: an adobe house with walls 3ft/1m thick dating from 1842; now a museum of local history spanning the years from 1830 to 1970.

Casa Soberanes

Another adobe building constructed in 1827 during the period of Mexican rule; today it houses an exhibition on the decades between 1830 and 1850. The two famous Monterey cypresses grow in the garden in front of the house.

Custom House

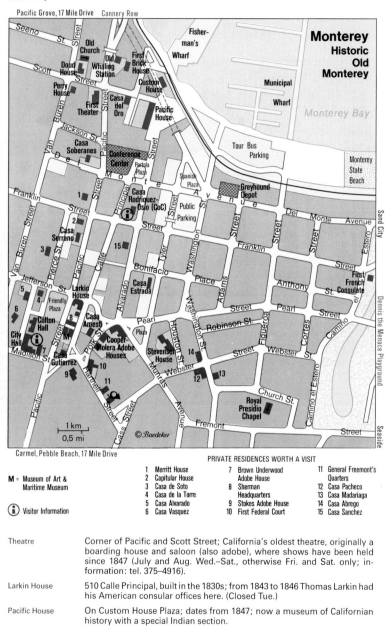

Pacific Grove, 17 Mile Drive   Cannery Row

Monterey
Historic
Old
Monterey

Fisher-
man's
Wharf

Seeno St.

Old
Church

Doud
House

Old
Whaling
Station

First
Brick
House

Custom
House

Municipal

Scott

Perry
House

Casa
del
Oro

Pacific
House

Wharf

Monterey Bay

First
Theater

Jackson St.

Casa
Soberanes

Conference
Center

Portola
Plaza

Spanish
Plaza

Tour Bus
Parking

Monterey
State
Beach

Franklin
Street

Casa
Rodriguez-
Osio (CoC)

Public
Parking

Greyhound
Depot

Del Monte   Avenue

Sand City

Casa
Serrano

Franklin

15

Bonifacio
Place

Anthony

First
French
Consulate

St.

Larkin
House

Casa
Estrada

Pearl   Street

Jefferson St.

Pierce St.

Friendly
Plaza

Robinson St.

Webster

Colton
Hall

Casa
Amesti

Plaza

Camino

City
Hall

M

Cooper
Molera Adobe
Houses

Stevenson
House

14

Dennis the Menace Playground

Madison St.

Casa
Gutierrez

10

12

13

Royal
Presidio
Chapel

Church St.

Camino el Estero

Seaside

Fremont

Street

1 km

0,5 mi

© *Baedeker*

Carmel, Pebble Beach, 17 Mile Drive

M = Museum of Art &
Maritime Museum

ℹ️ Visitor Information

PRIVATE RESIDENCES WORTH A VISIT

1 Merritt House	7 Brown Underwood	11 General Freemont's
2 Capitular House	Adobe House	Quarters
3 Casa de Soto	8 Sherman	12 Casa Pacheco
4 Casa de la Torre	Headquarters	13 Casa Madariaga
5 Casa Alvarado	9 Stokes Adobe House	14 Casa Abrego
6 Casa Vasquez	10 First Federal Court	15 Casa Sanchez

Theatre   Corner of Pacific and Scott Street; California's oldest theatre, originally a
                    boarding house and saloon (also adobe), where shows have been held
                    since 1847 (July and Aug. Wed.–Sat., otherwise Fri. and Sat. only; in-
                    formation: tel. 375–4916).

Larkin House   510 Calle Principal, built in the 1830s; from 1843 to 1846 Thomas Larkin had
                    his American consular offices here. (Closed Tue.)

Pacific House   On Custom House Plaza; dates from 1847; now a museum of Californian
                    history with a special Indian section.

Old factories, new uses – Monterey's famous Cannery Row

530 Houston Street, built for a rich family; the Scottish writer stayed here for four months while visiting his future bride; numerous Stevenson memorabilia. (Closed Wed.)

Robert Louis Stevenson House

The Monterey Presidio, now the Defense Language Institute; artefacts and dioramas illustrating the history of Presidio Hill under the Indians, Mexicans, Spanish and Americans. Entry free.

Presidio
Pacific Street

The Royal Presidio Chapel (San Carlos Cathedral, 550 Church Street) is the only remaining Presidio chapel in California; it has been in continuous use since 1795. Note the very fine ornate façade.

Monterey has two museums: the Monterey Peninsula Museum of Art with collections of Californian, Indian and Asiatic art as well as temporary exhibitions of photographs (559 Pacific Street; tel. 372–7591); and the Allen Knight Maritime Museum illustrating the maritime history of the area (550 Calle Principal; tel. 375–2553).

Museums

Fisherman's Wharf with its shops and reasonably priced restaurants is also worth a visit.

Fisherman's Wharf

★★Monterey Bay Aquarium

The superb Monterey Bay Aquarium, opened in 1984, occupies the site of the old Hovden Cannery, one of the largest of the eighteen in Cannery Row. The architecture of the elaborate aquarium complex, the biggest of its kind in the USA, was adapted from that of the former factory which stood here from 1916 to 1980 (though abandoned after 1972). The aquarium stands right on the edge of the rocky bay. There is a restaurant with a sea view and an oyster bar.

Location
886 Cannery Row

Opening times
daily (except Christmas Day)
10am–6pm

Monterey

Entrance fee
(expensive)

The marvellously well-equipped aquarium focuses on the exceptionally rich marine life of Monterey Bay, each aspect of which – the coastal formations, marine vegetation, fish and other forms of marine life, and birds of sea and shore – can be observed in several different ways: through the glass walls of tanks, through telescopes, macroscopes and microscopes, and even by means of underwater video cameras remotely controlled by the observer.

In the larger aquaria experts in diving gear provide on the spot commentaries broadcast over loudspeakers from amongst the flora and fauna.

The complex comprises 80 pools (some are two storeys deep) and 20 galleries both under cover and in the open. They contain about 6000 specimens representing nearly 60 species (sharks and other large fish, sea-otters, giant octopuses, crustaceans, starfish, etc.).

A "Habitat Path" guides visitors around the various sections on the main floor, the most impressive of which are the so-called "Monterey Bay Habitats" (a stretch of coast 30yd/27.5m long), the "Kelp Forest" (a giant tank, 28ft/8.5m high, holding 280,000 gall/1.26 million litres of seawater), and the "Great Tide Pool".

The large "Marine Mammals Gallery" contains lifelike models of mammals which inhabit the bay, including whales, dolphins, sea-lions and seals. Sea-otters, an endangered species, are bred in the aquarium and can be seen romping about in a special two-storey pool.

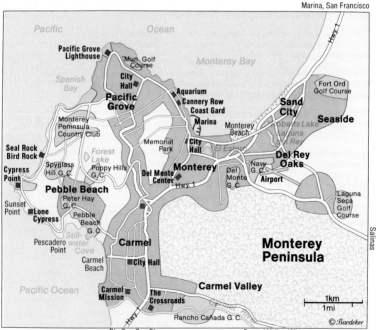

The "Lone Cypress" – one of many scenic features on 17 Mile Drive

The section called "Mexico's Secret Sea", opened in 1989, explores the tropical undersea world of the Gulf of California (complete with 300 of its more unusual denizens). "Jewels of the Pacific", opened in the same year, does the same for a spectrum of the Pacific Ocean's marine life and underwater formations.

Surroundings

Nearby Pacific Grove (population 15,000) boasts numerous Victorian houses, a natural history museum, and the Asilomar Conference Centre.

Pacific Grove

The 3¾mile/6km-long Ocean View Boulevard (with delightful footpaths) overlooks the rocky coast. South of Monterey are Pebble Beach and Del Monte, both with near palatial villas and golf courses which are among the most beautiful on the Monterey peninsula.

If heading for Carmel (see entry), only a mile or two from Monterey on the south side of the Monterey peninsula, it is well worth taking the roundabout route known as "17 Mile Drive"; it offers marvellous views. Starting at Pacific Grove Gate it continues south along the coast, passing for part of its way through the Del Monte Forest in which many large villas are situated and which is particularly impressive on account of the large numbers of cypress trees and so-called Monterey pines.

★ 17 Mile Drive
Private Road
(Toll)
Information
Tel. 1–800–654–9300

Other features along the road include picturesque beaches, solitary rocks, the "Lone Cypress", Pebble Beach Golf Club and the "Lodge at Pebble Beach" (hotel).

Seal Rock and Bird Rock are home to colonies of many different types of gull; sea-lions and seals can often also be sighted. Cypress Lookout affords especially fine views along the Pacific Coast north and south.

Moscone Convention Center   I 9

Location
South of Market
Street, between
Howard and
Folsom Streets
Entrance:
777 Market Street

Situated south of Market Street and opened in 1981, the Moscone Center occupies a site of almost 12 acres/5ha bounded by 3rd, Howard, 4th and Folsom Streets. A venue for exhibitions and congresses it comprises a 243,000sq.ft/22,600sq.m exhibition hall (the largest column-free interior space in the USA), 41 conference rooms seating from 30 to 7000, and a ballroom. The new cultural, recreational and business complex in the adjacent Yerba Buena Gardens will, when complete, almost double this capacity.

Guided tours

Sat. 1pm from the Moscone Center entrance in Howard Street (information: tel. 558–3770).

Mount Tamalpais   G 31

Location
20 miles/32km
north

At 2700ft/820m Mount Tamalpais is the highest point in the immediate vicinity of San Francisco. From the top there is a magnificent view of the Golden Gate. The summit can be reached by car (via Golden Gate Bridge and US 101); the alternative is to park at the bottom and walk up one of the many footpaths.

The area around Mount Tamalpais is now nearly all Californian State Park territory, with large picnic areas and two camp sites. As in Muir Woods (see entry) a few miles further on, there are many redwood trees (*Sequoia sempervirens*) in evidence here.

★Muir Woods (Giant redwood grove)   G/H 31

Location
Mill Valley, CA
15 miles/24km
north

Route
Highway 101 and
California 1
Bus service via
Sausalito

Giant redwood trees thrive only in California and Oregon. The most famous and tallest specimens in the world grow in Muir Woods, only a few miles from San Francisco. The woods, designated a National Monument in 1908, are cared for by the National Park Service which runs a kiosk at the entrance where visitors can obtain all the information they need.

Muir Woods are named after the naturalist John Muir who, back in the 19th c., tried to persuade Americans to take an interest in nature conservation. He founded the Sierra Club in San Francisco, the first influential organisation concerned with ecology.

Redwoods

These woods cover 550 acres/223ha and contain many specimens of the famous giant redwood (*Sequoia sempervirens*), the trunks of which can be up to 20ft/6m across. They are found growing naturally only along the Pacific Coast, in a belt 540 miles/870km long and 30 miles/48km wide extending from south of Monterey (see entry) northward to the south-west corner of the state of Oregon. Here the heavy rainfall from November to April and mists morning and evening during the dry summer months ensure the humid conditions required for the growth of these massive trees. The tallest giant redwoods in Muir Woods reach a height of 240ft/73m. In the first hundred years they grow at a rate of about 1ft/30cm a year before slowing down thereafter. The oldest recorded giant redwood, which has since died, was estimated to be 2200 years old. The average age is between 400 and 800 years. The root system of these trees can extend outwards as much as 150ft/46m but never penetrates deeper than 20ft/6m.
Muir Woods has 6 miles/10km of footpaths, all well sign-posted. The generally cool damp conditions, even in summer, make warm clothing advisable.

Muir Woods: giant redwoods, the world's tallest trees

Museum of Modern Art

See San Francisco Museum of Modern Art

Museum of Money of the American West

See Bank of California

Museum of the City of San Francisco

This new museum is the first devoted exclusively to the city's history. Its collection consists of photographs, town plans, paintings and objects of civic interest such as the statue of the Goddess of Progress which graced the dome of the old City Hall destroyed in the 1906 earthquake.

Location
2801 Leavenworth
Ave. (3rd floor)

Open: Wed.–Sun. 11am–4pm. Entry free.

★Napa and Sonoma Valleys (Wine-growing areas)

Napa Valley and Sonoma Valley are the best-known and largest vine-growing areas in California. Even in Europe the excellent wines they produce have gained an increasing market share.

Location
43–53 miles/
70–85km north

Viticulture, introduced into California about 1825 by Spanish Franciscans, was subsequently developed to its present high standard by wine growers

Viticulture

87

Vineyards in Sonoma County

from Germany, Alsace, France, Hungary and Italy. The wineries north of the Bay are reckoned the best in the United States. Grapes are harvested from September through to the beginning of November. Altogether the Napa and Sonoma Valleys have nearly 150 wineries, much the same as in the whole of the rest of the state. There are now 5289 acres/2100ha of vineyards in the Sonoma Valley alone, a telling indication of the importance of this branch of agriculture in California.

Sonoma

Sonoma lies about 43 miles/70km north of San Francisco on US 12, a road which passes through delightful scenery. The place-name is not, as is often supposed, Spanish in origin but comes from a Wintun Indian word meaning "nose". Precisely why this name was chosen when the town was founded in 1835 remains obscure.

History

In contrast to Napa which claims no historical importance, Sonoma does have a place in Californian history. For a while in 1846 it was the state capital. Prior to that, Mariano Guadelupe Vallejo, who was born in Monterey (see entry) when it was capital of the Spanish colony of Alta California, had become Commander-in-Chief of the Mexican forces in the province after the Spanish yoke had been cast off. Between 1836 and 1846 he was the unchallenged ruler of North California, which he governed from Sonoma.

Increasing numbers of American settlers flocked to the province however, and on June 14th 1846 they took over Sonoma Barracks, arrested Vallejo and proclaimed an independent republic of California. This had its own flag, with a bear as its emblem, still occasionally seen flying in the state. But only a month later US troops took control of the whole of Alta California and put an end to the separatist dream.

Wineries

The Sonoma wineries are strung out along the CA 12 and CA 128 as they wend their way up the valley. The Buena Vista Cellars on the eastern outskirts of Sonoma were founded in 1857 by the Hungarian Count Agos-

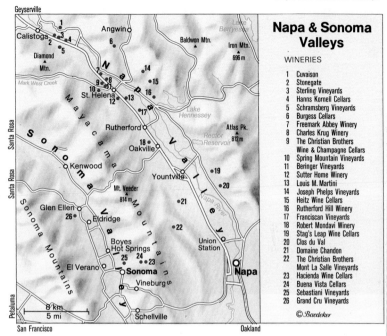

Geyserville

Napa & Sonoma Valleys

WINERIES

1 Cuvaison
2 Stonegate
3 Sterling Vineyards
4 Hanns Kornell Cellars
5 Schramsberg Vineyards
6 Burgess Cellars
7 Freemark Abbey Winery
8 Charles Krug Winery
9 The Christian Brothers
   Wine & Champagne Cellars
10 Spring Mountain Vineyards
11 Beringer Vineyards
12 Sutter Home Winery
13 Louis M. Martini
14 Joseph Phelps Vineyards
15 Heitz Wine Cellars
16 Rutherford Hill Winery
17 Franciscan Vineyards
18 Robert Mondavi Winery
19 Stag's Leap Wine Cellars
20 Clos du Val
21 Domaine Chandon
22 The Christian Brothers
   Mont La Salle Vineyards
23 Hacienda Wine Cellars
24 Buena Vista Winery
25 Sebastiani Vineyards
26 Grand Cru Vineyards

© Baedeker

San Francisco   Oakland

ton Haraszthy, generally considered the father of Californian viticulture (though the Franciscan Fathers were already growing grapes for their Communion wine as early as 1825). The cellars now belong to Hubertus von Wulffen, a German; excellent concerts take place here during the summer months.

The Sebastiani Vineyards and Winery are more recent in origin, dating from 1904, and are still owned by the Sebastiani family (guided tours between 10am and 5pm). The Haywood Winery can also be visited.

Among the best-known varieties, all deriving from European vines, are Chardonnay, Pinot Noir, Merlot, Johannisberg Riesling, Gewürztraminer and, in higher locations, Cabernet Sauvignon. The American Zinfandel is also cultivated.

Wine

In Sonoma itself it is possible to visit what remains of Vallejo's residence (on the plaza, corner of W. Spain Street/3rd Street West). Built in 1850–51 the greater part of it was destroyed by fire in 1867. The adobe barracks dating from 1834 where Vallejo's troops were stationed can also be seen (E. Spain Street/1st West Street). Other buildings of interest include the former Toscana Hotel and numerous mid 19th c. houses.

State Historic Park

Sonoma's Mission San Francisco Solano was the northernmost and last of the 21 set up by the Franciscans along the Californian coast. It fulfilled its intended purpose for barely a decade (1823 to 1833). The mission was first restored in 1909; archaeological digs still take place from time to time.

Near the Sonoma Valley community of Glen Ellen is the entrance to the Jack London State Park, named after the famous Californian author who died when only 40 years old. Close to the entrance stands the "House of

Jack London State Park

Sonoma Valley winery · Mission San Francisco Solano

Happy Walls'', built by his widow; about a mile further on are Jack London's grave and the still-impressive ruins of Wolf House, built by London himself but burned down before it could be occupied.

Santa Rosa

Santa Rosa (population 89,000) is situated at the northern end of the Sonoma Valley in the vine-growing area of Sonoma County – there are 100 or so vineyards in the near vicinity. Being only 53 miles/85km from San Francisco it is popular with those who, undeterred by the distance, prefer to live out of town and commute. Santa Rosa was made famous by Luther Burbank, noted American agronomist and breeder of new varieties of vegetable and fruit (Luther Burbank Memorial Gardens, corner of Sonoma and Santa Rosa Avenues. Open: daily 8am–5pm. Entry free).

Peanuts Museum

No. 1 Snoopy Place is the address of the villa owned by the well-known comic artist Charles M. Schulz. Of German origin, he was born in Minneapolis (MN) in 1922. His comic strip ''Peanuts'', with Charlie Brown, the beagle Snoopy, Lucy, Linus and co., first appeared in 1950 and has proved itself one of the most successful ever.

Napa

With a population of 53,000, Napa, some 13½ miles/22km east of Sonoma, is one of the largest Californian towns north of San Francisco. Founded in 1848 it bears the name of the Napa Indians, long since died out. Most of the wine produced in the Napa Valley as far north as Calistoga (see below) passes through Napa, but the town also has tanneries and light industrial and electronics businesses. The Napa Valley is exceedingly well sheltered, lying as it does between the Howell Mountains to the east and the Mayacama Mountains to the west.

Wineries

The principal Napa Valley wineries are found along the stretch of road from St Helena (see below) to Oakville and Rutherford: Mondavi, Beaulieu, Inglenook, Heitz and Louis Martini are all names highly regarded in Europe

One of the many wine vaults in Napa Valley

as well as in America. Other well-known vineyards – Beringer Brothers, Christian Brothers (owned by an Order of Catholic missionaries) and Charles Krug, founded in 1861 by a German and one of the oldest wineries in the valley – border the CA 128 north of St Helena. Further north still are the Hans Kornell Cellars and Schramsberg, one of the few American champagne producers. Cabernet Sauvignon is among the best of the red wines, Johannisberg Riesling among the best of the white.

In recent years some 50 or so Californian wineries have passed partly or wholly into foreign hands; they include Inglenook and Beaulieu (now British owned) and Beringer (now Swiss owned). Since 1970 the number of wine producers in the Napa Valley has grown from 30 to 200.

The ever-growing popularity of guided tours of the Wine Country, many of them laid on by the larger firms (about 2.5 million tourists a year), means that the Valley is acquiring more and more of a tourist atmosphere. Since 1989 the opportunity has existed to explore the area by rail, travelling in the comfort of real Pullman coaches operating on a stretch of the Napa Valley line. George Mortimer Pullman began building the famous luxury Pullman saloon and sleeping-cars in Chicago in 1858. In addition to vineyard visits and wine-tasting, gourmet meals are served in the elegant dining car on the 36 mile/58km journey from Napa to St Helena and back.

Tourism

Should wine cellars and vineyards not be enough, a short stay in St Helena (population 5000), about 18 miles/29km north-west of Napa, can be included in the itinerary. Here Robert Louis Stevenson (see also below – Calistoga) is commemorated in the Silverado Museum; as well as first editions of his works it has manuscripts, photos and letters (open: Tue.–Fri. noon–4pm; entry free). Six large wineries – Beaulieu, Beringer, Inglenook, Hans Kornell, Charles Krug and Louis M. Martini – are located in or around this important little wine centre.

St Helena

Lake Berryessa	Lake Berryessa, about 12 miles/20km east of St Helena, was formed when the Monticello Dam was built. With 165 miles/265km of shoreline it offers good facilities for watersports.
Calistoga	Situated at the northern end of the Napa Valley, Calistoga was founded in 1859 by Sam Brannan who recognised the potential of its hot springs (the name Calistoga was coined from those of California and Saratoga, a well-known resort in New York State). Calistoga's popularity peaked in the 1870s; since then viticulture has become the mainstay of its economy.
Sharpsteen Museum	The Sharpsteen Museum in Calistoga's main street (1411 Washington Street) has photographs, dioramas and other exhibits documenting the town's early days when it was still a resort. Standing next to the museum is one of the cabins in which guests were accommodated at the time. Open: May–Oct. 10am–4pm, otherwise noon–4pm.
Mount St Helena	About 8 miles/13km north of Calistoga the 4266ft/1300m extinct volcano, Mount St Helena, rises high above the Napa Valley. Here in 1880 Robert and Fanny Stevenson spent part of their honeymoon (Robert Louis Stevenson State Park complete with a statue of the writer). The mountain, just off the CA 29, is one of the Mayacama range (named after the old Indian village of Miyakmah near Calistoga).
Old Faithful Geyser	About 1 mile/1.6km north of Calistoga, between the CA 128 and CA 29, California's own "Old Faithful" geyser sends water spouting 65ft/20m into the air. Occasionally its normally regular rhythm (every 40 minutes) becomes disrupted. Open: in summer daily 9am–6pm, otherwise until 5pm.
Petrified redwoods	5 miles/9km west of Calistoga there is a petrified redwood forest and associated museum (reached by Petrified Forest Road; open: daily 9am–6pm in summer, otherwise 9am–5pm).

National Maritime Museum   G 7

Location
In Aquatic Park
at the end of
Polk Street

Bus routes
19, 30, 32, 47

Cable car 60

The National Maritime Museum pays homage to the seafarers who, together with their ships, made such a vital contribution to the growth of population and trade on the West Coast of America. Craft dating back to the early history of California and a wide range of nautical paraphernalia provide a lively insight into the life and work of those who built and sailed the ships.

The museum is split between a number of different sites.

Maritime Museum

Opening times
Wed.–Sun.
10am–5pm

Closed
Christmas Day
New Year's Day

Guided tours
daily 12.30 and
3.30pm

The building itself dates from 1939. In the first twelve or so years of its life it served various purposes before being converted into the National Maritime Museum. Today it houses models of the many different kinds of ships which passed regularly through the Golden Gate – passenger ships, cargo ships and men-of-war.

    The library, located on the upper floor (open: Wed.–Fri. only), contains old newspaper cuttings, books and pamphlets relating to Californian maritime history as well as ship's logs, maps and charts. The photograph archive has more than 100,000 prints of sailing ships, steamers, West Coast harbours and views of San Francisco's constantly changing port. Literature on the history of navigation on the West Coast of America is available from the bookstall.

View of the exterior of the National Maritime Museum

The sailing vessel "Balclutha", restored for the National Maritime Museum

National Maritime Museum

Historic ships

Opening times
May–Sept.
daily 10am–6pm
Oct.–Apr.
daily 10am–5pm

Entrance fee

Five historic ships belonging to the musuem are moored at Hyde Street Pier:

"Eureka": a paddle-driven ferry which was in operation from 1890 to 1957. It carried passengers between Marin County and Oakland. In its day it was the largest passenger ferry in the world.

"C. A. Thayer": a sailing schooner built in 1895. First used in the timber trade it then carried salted salmon and finally, up until 1950, was used for cod-fishing in the Bering Sea.

"Wapama": a steam schooner of 1915. Carried mainly timber but also had some passenger cabins.

"Alma": a two-masted lighter built in 1891 for carrying coal, sand, timber, etc. in San Francisco Bay and the adjoining rivers; in use until 1958.

"Hercules": a deep-sea tug which operated from West Coast harbours from 1907 to 1962.

Historic ships at other moorings:

"Balclutha" (Pier 43): a steel-hulled sailing vessel built in England in 1886, in use until 1954, and now restored to its original state. Mainly used to carry coal round Cape Horn to San Francisco and grain back to Europe. Open: daily 9am–6pm (entrance fee).

"USS Pampanito" (Pier 45): a US submarine, built in 1943; saw action in the Pacific during the Second World War. Open: Mon.–Thur. 9am–6pm, Fri.–Sun. until 9pm (entrance fee).

Navy/Marine Corps/Coast Guard Museum

Location
Treasure Island

Bus route
AC Transit from
Bus Station,
Mission Street
and 1st Street
Infomation about
departures, tel.
653–3535

Construction of the Navy/Marine Corps/Coast Guard Museum was started at the time of the United States Bicentennial Celebrations. With the aid of displays, documents and pictures the museum records the role of the US Navy and Marine Corps in the Pacific. A special attraction is the huge mural by Lowell Nesbitt.
Open: daily 10am–3.30pm.

Wonderful views of San Francisco's skyscrapers are obtained during the drive over the San Francisco–Oakland Bridge and especially from Treasure Island. Treasure Island, it should be said, is man-made. It is part of Yerba Buena Island which was reclaimed from the sea in a project carried out for the 1939 Golden Gate Exhibition.

★Nob Hill   H 8 (I 4/5)

Location
West of Chinatown

Cable car
61 (California St.)

Nob Hill, rising to more than 330ft/100m, is one of the smartest districts of San Francisco. Prior to the 1906 earthquake it was where the most prosperous San Franciscans lived and it still boasts many palatial houses.
Three explanations are offered for the name. It may derive from the word "Nabob", which in India means a rich man; alternatively from the word "snob"; or perhaps – and this seems most likely – it comes from the word "knob" meaning a knoll or rounded hill. Originally the hill was called "California Street Hill" after the street leading up it from the city's financial quarter.

The area began to attract San Francisco's rich – bankers, industrialists and newspaper owners – at the end of the 1850s. They were joined some 15 or

On Nob Hill – the premises of the Pacific Union Club

20 years later by the new wave of railroad millionaires, among whom were Charles Crocker, Leland Stanford, Mark Hopkins and Collis Huntingdon. As one book about San Francisco put it, they "didn't exactly own California but its interests certainly lay in their hands".

Among the many fine buildings on Nob Hill the following are of particular note:

Stouffer Stanford Court Hotel (905 California Street): originally a luxurious private residence built in 1911 and converted into a hotel in 1972. Up until the earthquake this was the site of Stanford Villa.

Mark Hopkins Inter-Continental Hotel (999 California Street): site of Hopkins Villa until it was destroyed in the earthquake. The 20-storey hotel was built some years later, in 1925. Its "Top of the Mark" bar enjoys one of the best views over the city.

Fairmont Hotel and Tower (950 Mason Street): paid for by James G. Fair, the "Silver King". It was gutted by fire just before its opening in 1906 and so took another year to complete. The foyer ranks as one of the finest public rooms in San Francisco. The external lift added to the tower in 1962 is another special attraction.

Pacific Union Club (1000 California Street): San Francisco's most exclusive gentlemen's club. The villa it occupies was built in 1886 by James Flood, another "Silver King", and renovated 26 years later.

University Club (800 Powell Street), on the corner of California Street, originally the site of Stanford's stables; the house, a sort of Florentine town mansion, was built in 1912.

Grace Cathedral (see entry)

Masonic Memorial Auditorium (1111 California Street): one of Nob Hill's few modern buildings, erected in 1958. Several 1920s Art Deco houses also survive, e.g. 1250 Jones Street, 1298 Sacramento Street, 1000 Mason Street and 1100 Sacramento Street.

The land for Huntingdon Park (California Street, between the Pacific Union Club and Grace Cathedral – see entry) was given to the city in 1915 by Collis Huntingdon's widow. It is now one of the most beautiful small parks in San Francisco.

North Beach (Nightclub and discoland)   H/I 7/8 (I/J 3/4)

Location
Broadway,
Columbus Avenue,
Washington
Square

Bus
15

North Beach – a misleading name if ever there was one, there is definitely no beach here now – is one of the liveliest parts of San Francisco; its streets throng with immigrant peoples from all corners of the globe.

San Francisco's nightclub and discoland is reached by continuing north along Grant Avenue, the main street running through Chinatown (see entry). North Beach starts beyond Columbus Avenue and Broadway.

This is the place to enjoy the city's night life which, since the clubs and bars with their brightly lit neon signs hardly ever close, goes on almost continuously 24 hours a day. Girls cavort in various states of undress, there are pornographic cinemas and live theatre shows, and jazz clubs which regularly feature leading jazz musicians. The district also boasts a number of discos famous throughout the city.

From the corner of Kearny and Columbus Streets there is an especially fine view of the Transamerica Pyramid (see entry).

North Beach – San Francisco's night-time playground

Washington Square, further along Columbus Avenue, lies at the centre of San Francisco's Italian quarter, a "Little Italy" markedly more colourful and more obviously Italian than similar areas in other American cities. Home to over 50,000 Italians, a glance at the shops and restaurants is enough to show just how vigorous the Italian way of life remains here. Italians have played a greater role in the history of San Francisco than perhaps any other European ethnic group. Washington Square was also where the Hippies and Flower People used to gather in the 1960s and 1970s and from where the psychedelic movement spread.

Washington Square

Telegraph Hill with Coit Tower (see entries) is also part of North Beach.

Oakland

I 32

Oakland is situated on hilly ground rising to 1750ft/533m at the eastern end of the San Francisco-Oakland Bay Bridge. Although little remains of them now, oak forests and redwood groves once grew near the bay; at one time there was a logging camp here. When in 1852 the gold prospectors arrived and founded the city, they chose to name it after the trees. Oakland grew in status when it became the terminus of the transcontinental railroad. That same year Oakland's Mayor Merritt created the city-centre lake which bears his name. Development of the port, with the construction of piers and canalisation of the estuary, reflected the major role planned for Oakland as a place where all forms of transport converged. In 1991 entire districts of the city were destroyed by fire. Today Oakland has a population of some 347,000.

Location
7½ miles/12km
north-east of
San Francisco

BART station
Lake Merritt

Bus
AC Transit Line A

Rivalry between San Francisco and Oakland is intense and their respective inhabitants the butt of the others' none too kindly humour. On the whole Oakland has little to offer sightseers.

Following the earthquake of 1906, the devastating effects of which Oakland was largely spared, the influx of people from San Francisco was such that, between 1900 and 1910, the city's population doubled. In the 1920s

Economy

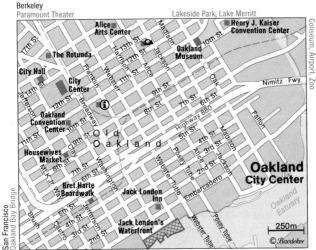

Oakland's industry flourished and large office blocks were built. The Second World War brought further important developments. In particular the port installations were improved so that, in the 1950s, Oakland, with considerably more foresight than San Francisco, was better prepared for the container revolution and had soon overtaken San Francisco as the West Coast's principal container port. As a result 1000 haulage companies set up in Oakland. There are also several large ship-yards and about 1600 factories.

Black Panthers

As Oakland grew it attracted many blacks, particularly from the southern United States; by 1970 they accounted for about a third of the city's population. It was here in 1966 that Bobby Seale and Huey Newton founded the Black Panther movement. Their followers were involved in several clashes with the police and various acts of violence before militancy gave way to moderation.

Lake Merritt

Lake Merritt, a salt-water lagoon on which boating is allowed, occupies 150 acres/64ha in the centre of the city. It is surrounded by Lakeside Park among the attractions of which are the Children's Fairyland and a Japanese Garden. Oakland Museum stands in large grounds at the south-west end of the lake.

Bret Harte
Broadwalk,
Jack London
Square

Of various writers who grew up in Oakland the best known are Bret Harte and Jack London (see Famous People). The former is commemorated by Bret Harte Broadway and the latter by Jack London Square, at the lower end of Broadway, where there is a bust of the writer. As well as downing his whiskey in "Heinhold's First and Last Chance Saloon", London also penned many of his short stories there. Next to it stands the reconstructed Klondike cabin in which he spent one winter.

Adjacent to Jack London Square, at the foot of Alice Street, is Jack London Village with shops, restaurants and a marina.

Gertrude Stein

Though born in neighbouring San Francisco, the writer Gertrude Stein was another who spent part of her youth in Oakland. In the early 1880s she lived here with her parents on a farm. Her famous remark "When you get there, there is no there there", often quoted in connection with Los Angeles, expressed the disappointment she felt when she returned after forty years in Europe to find the house had gone.

J. Miller Park

The Joaquin Miller Park is named after another Californian author who lived in Oakland.

Oakland Zoo

The zoo is situated 7 miles/11km south of the city centre off Highway 580 (open: daily; tel. 510–632–9523).

Paramount
Theatre of
the Arts

Anyone visiting Oakland on the first or third Saturday of the month should be sure not to miss the guided tour, starting 10am, of the Paramount Theatre of the Arts (2025 Broadway, tel. 510–893–2300). The theatre is one of the last 1920s Art Deco picture houses remaining in the United States. Designed by Timothy L. Pflueger it is now used for concerts by the Oakland Symphony Orchestra.

★Oakland Museum

Location
1000 Oak Street
Tel. 510–273–3401

Oakland Museum, at the south-west end of Lake Merritt, has notable collections devoted to Californian history, natural history and folk customs. It stands in extensive grounds where visitors can stroll.

Opening times
Wed.–Sat.
10am–5pm
Sun. noon–7pm

The origins of the museum go back to 1910 when the Oakland Public Museum was founded, followed a few years later by the Oakland Art Gallery. The present museum, built largely below ground on a sloping site,

Sculpture by a Californian artist: Fletcher Benton's "M"

Oakland Museum: room in the Department of Californian History

Octagon House

Guided tours
Wed.–Fri. 2pm

Entry free

was designed by the well-known architect Kevin Roche. It is the only museum devoted exclusively to the history and culture of California, a restriction dictated in the first instance by economic considerations – Oakland lacked the resources of other museums to make expensive purchases in the art market.

The upper storey, through which the museum is entered, contains works by Californian painters. Below it is a great exhibition gallery devoted to California's history. The lower floor – the floors are stepped, terrace fashion, rather than one on top of the other – focuses on the natural history of California and includes an auditorium.

In addition to painters, Californian photographers are also well represented, among them Ansel Adams, Dorothea Lange, Edward Weston and Edward Muybridge.

Octagon House (Museum)   G 8

Location
2645 Gough Street
Corner of Union
Street

Bus
41

In the late 1850s San Francisco was gripped by a short-lived vogue for octagonal houses with dormer windows and roof lanterns. It was triggered by a book recommending the design as making for healthier living. Today only two such houses remain and only one, Octagon House, built in 1861, can be visited (guided tours: 2nd Sun. and 4th Thur. of month, noon–3pm; entry free).

Octagon House is undoubtedly a curiosity. It is nowadays the Californian headquarters of the National Society of Colonial Dames in America. The items on display are something of an anachronism as far as San Francisco is concerned. Most date from the American colonial period long before the city was founded.

The Old Mint – one of the buildings that withstood the 1906 earthquake

Old Mint

The Old Mint, erected between 1873 and 1874, was one of the few buildings in the Mission Street area not only to withstand the 1906 earthquake but to do so unscathed.

Several of its rooms have today been restored to their appearance in the 19th c., most notably the director's office.

Exhibits include a pyramid of gold bars in a circular safe, numerous privately minted coins from San Francisco's early days, photographs and works of art.

There are also temporary exhibitions from time to time. Visitors can mint their own souvenir using a press made in 1869.

Location
5th Street and
Mission Street

Opening times
Mon.–Fri.
10am–4pm

Closed
public holidays

Entry free

Old St Mary's Church

See Chinatown

Pacific Stock Exchange

The Pacific Stock Exchange was founded in 1873. Its present buildings, designed by the architects Miller and Pflueger, date from 1930 (as the Art Deco adornment unequivocally testifies). The two huge sculptures "Earth's Fruitfulness" and "Man's Inventive Genius" are by Ralph Stackpole.

Location
Corner of Pine
Street and
Sansome Street

Buildings of the Pacific Stock Exchange

Excursion boats at Pier 39

During trading hours visitors armed with a recommendation from one of San Francisco's stockbroking firms can observe the hectic activity on the floor of the Exchange from the gallery above.

★Pier 39 (Shopping and leisure centre)   H 7

Location
East of Fisherman's Wharf

Buses
19, 30

Cable car
59

Since its opening in 1978 this complex of 130 shops and numerous restaurants on the site of a derelict pier close to Fisherman's Wharf (see entry) has proved a great attraction. Pier 39 itself was completely rebuilt using timber from old ships; nearby jetties were demolished to create room for small craft moorings.

On both levels of the more than 1000ft/300m-long pier all is bustle and activity. Entertainment of one sort or another is virtually continuous throughout the day and there is always an enticing array of goods on display.

Magnificent views of San Francisco's skyscrapers are obtained from the end of the pier and from the restaurant jutting right out over the bay. Pier 39 is also the venue for a unique film show called "San Francisco Experience" (see Practical Information, Cinema).

Pioneer Hall (Museum)   G 9

Location
456 McAllister St.

Pioneer Hall, near the Civic Centre (see entry), houses the museum and library of the Society of Californian Pioneers, devoted chiefly to the early

View of San Francisco and yachts at Pier 39 ▶

Point Reyes National Seashore

Opening times Mon.–Fri. 10am–4pm	(pre-1869) history of California. There are historical documents and exhibits of various kinds, including a number of coaches.
Closed Public holidays	Scholars researching the history of California are allowed access to the comprehensive library and large photograph collection.

★Point Reyes National Seashore

Location and history	Point Reyes, 30 miles/48km north of San Francisco on Highway CA 1, was declared a National Seashore in 1962. It forms part of the Golden Gate National Recreation Area, the southern extremity of which is in San Francisco itself. It was on this peninsula, in 1579, that Sir Francis Drake set foot 41 years before the Pilgrim Fathers arrived in Plymouth. Although Drake claimed the land for the English Crown, his countrymen took little interest in the West of the newly discovered continent. 24 years later, on January 6th – Epiphany – 1603, the Spanish seafarer Don Sebastian Vizcaino landed here too, christening the peninsula La Punta de los Reyes (Kings' Point).
"Earthquake Way"	Point Reyes is situated at the western end of the San Andreas Fault, cause of all the earthquakes in the region. "Earthquake Way", a ½ mile/1km-long trail starting from the Bear Valley Visitor Centre, offers graphic evidence of movements of the earth's crust (e.g. sections of a fence, once joined, but now five metres apart).
Nature reserve	Countless sea birds overwinter in the Point Reyes coastal reserve. Several varieties of red deer inhabit the woods, as do foxes. Recently an attempt has been made to re-introduce moose.
Grey whales	In December and January Californian grey whales appear off the peninsula, heading south on their migration from the Arctic to Baja California; they return north again in April and May. Point Reyes lighthouse, erected in 1870 (fog is more frequent here than on any other part of the Californian coast) makes an excellent lookout spot.
Footpaths and bridleways	The Bear Valley Visitor Center is the gateway to more than 75 miles/120km of hiking trails and bridleways leading to all parts of the coastal reserve. Maps and information about the condition and length of trails can be obtained at the Visitor Center (open: Thur.–Mon. only; tel. 663–1092). A Miwok Indian village (the Miwoks were the original inhabitants of the area) has been reconstructed near by.

Presidio (Park and Museum)   E 8

Location In the north-west at the Golden Gate	The name "Presidio" goes back to 1776 when Spanish troops first established a garrison here. The wooded stretch of land, a little less than 1sq.mile/2.2sq.km in area, lies at the northern extremity of the San Francisco peninsula, jutting out into the Pacific. At the moment it is the headquarters of the US 6th Army. Most of the park-like base, criss-crossed by roads, is open to the public and there are many fine views. The Officers' Club, an adobe building dating from 1776, is the sole remaining relic of Spanish days. A lowering the flag ceremony takes place every evening at 5pm.
Bus 28	
Guided tours Tel. 921–8193 in advance	
	Also in the grounds of the Presidio is the National Military Cemetery where more than 15,000 casualties of the First World War lie buried. An older gravestone commemorates "Pauline Tyler, Union Spy". She was an actress who spied for the Union side during the American Civil War, winning promotion to the rank of major.

The Presidio Army Museum occupies an old military hospital dating from the 1850s. It has exhibitions of relics and documents illustrating the part played by the military in the development of San Francisco. (Open: Tue.–Sun. 10am–4pm; closed Thanksgiving Day, Christmas Day and New Year's Day; entry free.)

Presidio Army Museum
Lincoln and Funston St.

★St Mary's Cathedral

G 9

St Mary's Cathedral, the third to bear this name, is by far the most impressive of San Francisco's churches, and well worth seeing.

Consecrated in 1971, it replaced the second St Mary's Cathedral, on Van Ness Avenue, which burned down in 1962. Erected on a site formerly occupied by a supermarket, the cathedral can seat a congregation of 2500.

The building was designed by local architects Angus McSweeney, Paul A. Ryan and John M. Lee in association with Pietro Belluschi of the Massachusetts Institute of Technology in Boston (Mass.) and Pier Luigi Nervi of Rome. It has a pillar-less nave and a 195ft/60m-high dome at the apex of which four narrow stained glass windows converge like great translucent pathways to form a multi-coloured cross. The windows symbolise the four elements, air (north), earth (south), fire (west) and water (east). The altar, at which the priest faces the congregation, is surrounded on three sides by seats.

Above it hang a cross and a shimmering baldachino made from 7000 aluminium rods perpetually in motion. The organ, built in Padua by the Ruffati brothers, is raised on a plinth, creating the effect of a piece of sculpture.

Location
Gough Street and Geary Street

Bus
38

Opening times
Mon.–Sun.
8.30am–5pm;
Sun. and public holidays
afternoons only

St Mary's Cathedral, one of the most impressive churches in the city

St Mary's Cathedral: cross and baldacchino made out of 7000 aluminium rods

The cathedral's openness towards the outside world is symbolised by great glass windows through which church and city seem to merge. The view to the south-west, with San Francisco's second highest hill, Twin Peaks (see entry), in the centre, is particularly impressive.

A school with three courtyards, a large auditorium and a council chamber form part of the cathedral complex.

San Francisco African-American Historical and Cultural Society   G 7

Location
Fort Mason,
Building C.
Marina Boulevard.

Buses
41, 47

San Francisco has the only museum west of the Mississippi devoted to the culture and history of America's blacks. It has permanent exhibitions of documents and pictures relating to the history of the blacks in California and the part played by blacks in the American Civil War (1861–65).

Temporary exhibitions are mounted featuring works by black artists, especially those based in and around San Francisco. Open: Wed.–Sun. noon–5pm; entry free. Guided tours can be arranged on request in advance (tel. 441–0640).

San Francisco Fire Department Pioneer Memorial Museum   F9

Location
655 Presidio
Avenue

Bus 38

The massive doors of the Fire Department's museum (ring the bell at the fire station if they are closed) conceal a remarkable collection of photographs, equipment and documents from San Francisco's various fire brigades, especially the Volunteer Fire Brigade which was in existence from 1849 to 1866.

Much space is given over to documents relating to events during the disastrous blaze which followed the 1906 earthquake.

Opening times
Thur.–Sun.
1–4pm

There is also a special exhibition devoted to Lillie Hitchcock Coit; she financed the building of Coit Tower on Telegragh Hill (see entry) as a memorial to the fire brigade and was herself an honorary member of the brigade.

Closed
Public holidays

★★San Francisco Museum of Modern Art

I9 (J5)

The San Francisco Museum of Modern Art occupies a brand new building, opened as recently as January 1995, in Third Street opposite the Yerba Buena Gardens and Center for the Arts, having previously been housed in the War Memorial Veterans' Building to the west of Civic Center Plaza. With its distinctive circular tower in black and silver-grey striped granite, the imaginatively conceived red brick building designed by Swiss architect Mario Botta, a pupil of Le Corbusier and Louis Kahn, has quickly become a new San Francisco landmark. Having double the amount of exhibition space compared with the old building, the museum is now among the largest of its kind in America, second only to New York's Museum of Modern Art.

Opening times
Tue., Wed., Fri.
10am–5pm; Thur.
9am–9pm; Sat.,
Sun. 11am–5pm

Closed
Mon. and
public holidays

Entrance fee
(Free on 1st
Tue. of month)

Known prior to 1976 simply as the San Francisco Museum of Art, the museum is a private institution, unlike the three other major museums of art in San Francisco, the Asian Art Museum and M. H. de Young Memorial Museum in Golden Gate Park, and the California Palace of the Legion of Honor (see entries). Although its origins go back to the 1890s it was set on a firm footing only in 1916, thanks to the efforts of the San Francisco Art Association.

The avant-garde artist Frank Stella's "Khurasan Gate" (1969)

The museum was originally housed in the Palace of Fine Arts, a building erected in the Presidio for the Panama-Pacific Exposition and where the Exploratorium is now to be found. In 1925 it moved from these premises, which were gradually falling into disrepair, and was forced to put its collections into store for ten years until offered the use of a floor in the War Memorial Veterans' Building, which belongs to the city. Until a museum of modern art opened in Los Angeles in 1986, San Francisco's was the only one of its kind on the West Coast.

Naturally enough, Californian artists, not all of whom are well known, are singled out for attention, especially those American painters and sculptors who have made the West Coast their cultural home, such as Mark Rothko, Clyfford Still, Robert Motherwell, Jackson Pollock, Philip Guston and Sam Francis. Still, who died in 1981, presented the museum with 28 of his large-scale abstract paintings, and Guston gave several works to the museum before his death in 1980. Richard Dieberkorn, an internationally renowned Californian painter, has already made major gifts.

20th c. West Coast art

The museum's permanent collections now contain works by nearly every important modern European and American artist. But as far as European art is concerned, there is no real comparison with the Museum of Modern Art in New York either in terms of quantity or quality.

Art from Europe and the USA

Henri Matisse is particularly well represented, with nine paintings. George Braque's wonderful masterpiece "Le Guéridon" can also be seen. In 1980 the Josef Albers collection was greatly enhanced by the gift of seven more works. Among the German artists are Max Ernst, George Grosz, Hans Harting, Karl Hofer, Ernst Ludwig Kirchner, Franz Marc, Max Pechstein, Hans Purrmann, Kurt Schwitters and Fritz Winter. There are works by the Russian artists Alexej Jawlensky and Wassily Kandinsky. As for the French, the most notable are Pierre Bonnard, Paul Cézanne, Jean Dubuffet, Fernand Léger, Camille Pisarro and George Rouault. There are also works by the Spanish artists Joan Miró and Pablo Picasso.

The museum possesses works by the sculptors Alexander Archipenko, Hans Arp, Constantin Brâncusi, Jacob Epstein, Henri Laurens, Jacques Lipchitz, Marino Marini and Henry Moore.

Sculpture

As well as the American artists mentioned above, the museum exhibits the work of many others who have caught the public eye in the last few decades; they include Stuart Davis, Jim Dine, Helen Frankenthaler, Arshile Gorky, Adolphe Gottlieb, Robert Indiana, Elsworth Kelly, William de Kooning, Kenneth Noland, Georgia O'Keeffe, Claes Oldenburg, Ad Reinhardt, Frank Stella and Mark Tobey.

Avant-garde

The museum also has a large collection of photographs. Especially noteworthy are the several hundred original prints by Ansel Adams, who died in 1984.

Photograph collection

★San Francisco–Oakland Bay Bridge

J/K 8

The "Bay Bridge" links the city with Oakland (see entry) and the towns on the east side of the Bay. It was opened in 1936, six months before the Golden Gate Bridge (see entry). The bridge is 8 miles/13km long, making it one of the longest steel bridges in the world. It consists of two interconnected suspension bridges on the San Francisco side, a tunnel through Yerba Buena Island, and a lattice-work bridge on the Oakland side. Damage incurred during the earthquake in October 1989 caused the closure of the bridge for some considerable time.

Toll
$1; no charge for cars with at least 4 occupants

◄ Tom Holland's "McAdoo" (1981)

The Bay Bridge, looking towards San Francisco

The Bay Bridge does not quite match the Golden Gate Bridge for scenic quality; but the view of it from the quay where the ferries depart for Sausalito (see entry) and Larkspur, to the right of the Ferry Building tower (see entry), is particularly fine.

San Francisco Shopping Center

I 6

Location
Market Street
and 5th Street.

This, the most recent of San Francisco's many shopping centres (the others being Ghirardelli Square, Pier 39, The Cannery, Embarcadero Center, The Anchorage and Crocker Galleria, see entries), is unquestionably the most imposing. Located only three blocks away from Union Square, the nine-storey building has a 164ft/50m-high atrium and six spiral escalators (a Japanese innovation installed here for the very first time). The architects, the San Francisco firm of Whisler-Petri, have made extensive use of Italian marble, green granite and glass. The Center, which cost $140m to build, contains about 100 shops.

San Francisco Zoological Gardens

B 13

Location
Sloat & Skyline
Avenues at the
end of the Great
Highway

MUNI
Line L

When first established in 1889 the zoo was in Golden Gate Park; it moved to its present location in 1929. Now one of the six most important zoos in the United States, it was modelled on Hamburg's Hagenbeck Zoo.

The chief attractions are the snow leopards, polar bears, elephants, pigmy hippos, white rhinos and the monkeys which inhabit an island of their own.

A new primate center was added in 1985.

There is also a children's zoo, open daily from 11am to 4pm, where children are able to play with young animals and to feed them. They can also go for rides on giant tortoises and on roundabouts.

Opening times
daily 10am–5pm
Free on 1st
Wed. of month

★Sausalito   H 32

Formerly a fishing village on San Francisco Bay, Sausalito, at the northern end of the Golden Gate Bridge, took its name from the first ranch to be established there, called Rancho Saucelito. "Saucelito" – the old spelling was kept until 1900 – is a Spanish word meaning "little grove of willows"; but there are no willows there today. Where once whalers and trading vessels moored, nowadays the harbour is full of houseboats; in fact they are a real feature of Sausalito.

Narrow winding lanes, many of them linked by wooden steps, help make Sausalito especially attractive. While the bulk of the 7000-strong population are San Francisco commuters, artists have established something of a colony in the upper part of the town directly overlooking the Bay. Most of Sausalito's shops are on Bridgeway and Princess Street.

From Sausalito there are beautiful views of San Francisco, particularly when, with the sun shining in Sausalito, early morning mist still shrouds the city, leaving only the tops of the skyscrapers visible.

Sausalito has the somewhat unusual distinction of having launched several healthier living crusades upon the wider world. It was the first place to have a no-smoking day and claims to be the first cholesterol-free town in the USA, in rivalry with Palm Springs.

Location
8 miles/13km north
of San Francisco

Bus
Golden Gate bus,
to Market Street
and 7th Street

Ferries
Golden Gate
Ferry Pier and
White Fleet Pier
41 (Fisherman's
Wharf), Pier 1
at Ferry
Building

A characteristic sight at Sausalito: the houseboat colony

Sigmund Stern Grove (Amphitheatre)   C 13

Location
Sloat Boulevard
and 19th Avenue

MUNI station
Line L to Sunset
Boulevard, then
change to bus 18

Sigmund Stern Grove is a natural amphitheatre in the midst of conifer and eucalyptus woods.

On Sunday afternoons at 2pm from mid June to mid August free musical events are put on here – concerts, operettas, musicals and the occasional opera and ballet. They are hugely popular and can be thoroughly recommended.

Pine Lake Park, close by, is a good place for picnics.

Skyscrapers

San Francisco's ten tallest buildings are all located in the city's business quarter. In future no further skyscrapers are to be allowed outside this area; even within it, no building taller than the Transamerica Pyramid (see entry) is likely to gain approval.

1. Transamerica Pyramid, 600 Montgomery St. (see entry)   853ft/260m
2. Bank of America, 555 California St. (see entry)   778ft/232m
3. California Center, 345 California St.   724ft/217m
4. 101 California St.   600ft/180m
5. Five Fremont Center, 50 Fremont St.   600ft/180m
6. Citicorp Center, 1 Sansome St.   596m/179ft
7. One Embarcadero Center   568ft/173m
8. Four Embarcadero Center   568ft/173m
9. One Market Plaza   565ft/172m
10. Wells Fargo Building, 44 Montgomery St.   561ft/171m

Sonoma Valley

See Napa and Sonoma Valleys

Spreckels Mansion   G 8

Location
2080 Washington
Street (at
Lafayette Park)

Bus
48

Spreckels Mansion, situated two blocks west of Van Ness Avenue in the district known as Pacific Heights, is noteworthy both on account of the man who built it and for its architecture.

Adolph B. Spreckels was the son of Claus Spreckels, an immigrant from Hanover in Germany; Spreckels senior made his fortune as the "sugar king" of California. The architect of the mansion was George Applegarth, who took as his model a French Baroque palace.

Applegarth chose white stone for the building, which occupies the space of half a block. Three years later, in 1915, Spreckels entrusted him with an even more ambitious project, the design of the California Palace of the Legion of Honor (see entry) in Lincoln Park, which the millionaire and his wife bequeathed to the city.

Twenty-seven rooms have been turned into tourist accommodation (tel. 861–3008).

Spreckels' Mansion, built in the French Baroque style

★Stanford University Museum of Art

This museum, like the university itself, owes its creation to the generosity of Leland A. Stanford, one of the richest men in the San Francisco of his day, sometime President of the Central Pacific Railroad, Governor of California and United States Senator. In 1887 Stanford established a college on his farm at Palo Alto, which was to become the Stanford University of today. He founded the museum a few years later. Both were memorials to Stanford's son, who died at the age of 15 and who, during his childhood, had begun to collect mainly archaeological artefacts. In the museum are reconstructions of the boy's two rooms in the Stanford mansion on Nob Hill (see entry).

Though opened in 1894, the museum was completed only in 1905. Modelled on the National Museum of Athens, it has an Ionic colonnade, marble corridors and spacious exhibition galleries. Stanford and, after his death, his widow, purchased major collections for the museum. Among them were hundreds of archaeological items from Cyprus (from the Metropolitan Museum in New York), a collection of Indian burial offerings (from an exhibition in New Orleans), and the magnificent collection of Japanese and Chinese art formerly in the possession of Baron Ikeda (since this acquisition was made, the museum's Far Eastern collection has expanded to more than 7000 items).

The Stanford family collection of American paintings of the West (William Keith, Thomas Hill and Charles Nahl) is also in the museum which, for the past 20 years, has been concentrating on purchasing 19th and 20th c. European art. As a result there are now many important works of this period on show, up to and including paintings by Paul Klee. Beside the museum there is a garden containing numerous sculptures by Rodin.

Location
30 miles/48km south of San Francisco (Highway 101)

Opening times
Tue.–Fri. 10am–5pm, Sat. and Sun. 1–4pm

Closed
in Aug.

Entry free

Telegraph Hill

Buses
15 and 30 to
Columbus St. and
Union St. then
no. 39

Telegraph Hill, 295ft/90m high, is situated on the north side of the city centre. It is one of 43 hills in San Francisco. Rather like Montmartre in Paris, it has many artists' studios on its slopes, as well as prosperous middle class villas.

San Francisco is often likened to Rome and Lisbon as being "a city built on seven hills"; but that takes account of only the seven most prominent, of which Telegraph Hill is one (the others being Nob Hill (see entry), Rincon Hill, the Twin Peaks (see entry), Russian Hill, Lone Mountain and Mount Davidson).

Today there is no telegraph on Telegraph Hill; the name goes back to a so-called semaphore tower, erected on what was then a barren hilltop at the time of the Gold Rush. When ships were sighted coming in through the Golden Gate, their imminent arrival would be signalled to the merchants of Yerba Buena Cove, today's financial quarter. Thus forewarned they would be waiting at the anchorage even before the ships had made fast, so losing not a moment's trade. The signal tower was in use for only a few years however.

★ Coit Tower

Opening times
daily 9am–5pm

Coit Tower stands 500ft/150m above sea-level on the summit of Telegraph Hill. As well as having interesting murals, well worth seeing in their own right, the tower, though not as high as Twin Peaks (see entry), is still one of the best vantage points for views over San Francisco and the Bay. A lift ascends the 210ft/64m to the Perspex-glazed viewing platform. In clear weather it is possible to see as far as Mount Tamalpais (see entry).

One of San Francisco's 43 hills: Telegraph Hill, showing Coit Tower

The motif of the series of murals in the Coit Tower: working life in California

Temples to Mammon – San Francisco's business district

The tower is named after Lillie Hitchcock Coit (1843–1929), an honorary member of one of the fire fighting companies who, on her death, left $100,000 to the city. This paid for the erection of the tower in honour of the fire brigade. Constructed in 1934, it was designed by Arthur Brown jr., architect of the City Hall (see Civic Center) and other San Francisco buildings. There are many who claim to recognise in the shape of the free-standing columnar tower, the nozzle of a fire-hose.

The tower is decorated on the inside with sixteen monumental murals, the work of 25 painters and their nineteen assistants, undertaken as part of a work creation scheme during the Great Depression. The cycle of paintings has as its theme working life in California in 1934. The largest mural (34 × 10ft/10 × 3m), by Ralph Stackpole, depicts California's industries. In common with most of the murals it shows the strong influence of the Mexican artist Diego de Rivera, who lived in San Francisco for a period during the 1930s. Apart from those at ground-level, the murals inside the tower can only be viewed on Saturday mornings from 11am.

Murals

Coit Tower stands in Pioneer Park, a site which, until laid out as a park for the city's Centennial Celebrations held on Telegraph Hill, was little more than a barren stony hillside. There is a fine bronze statue of Christopher Columbus which is especially noteworthy. The plinth on which it stands was presented by the Italian port of Genoa.

Pioneer Park

Tiburon (Fishing Village)   H 31

Like Sausalito (see entry), Tiburon, meaning "shark", situated on a peninsula of the same name, still retains many features recalling its origins as a fishing village.

Location
15½ miles/25km
north-east of
San Francisco
(Highway 101)

The wooden houses on Main Street, Tiburon's principal thoroughfare, are today occupied by smart shops – boutiques, antique shops and galleries; there are also excellent fish restaurants. The narrow up-and-down streets lead to the modern part of the town and the villas of its mostly well-to-do inhabitants.

Ferries
Pier 43½ (Fisher-
man's Wharf)
May–Aug. 10am,
noon, 2, 3.45pm
last ferry from
Tiburon: 4.20pm

Tiburon is again like Sausalito in seeming much further removed from San Francisco than its 15½ miles/25km would suggest (the ferry crossing is even shorter, only half that distance). It remains in fact a different world.

★★Transamerica Pyramid   I 8 (J 5)

Since its completion in 1972 the Transamerica Pyramid, visible from almost anywhere in San Francisco, has become the city's latest symbol.

Location
600 Montgomery
Street

Situated at the heart of the financial district, the 48 storey-high pyramidal tower soars 853ft/260m into the air. It is owned by an insurance company which occupies a third of the total office space. The architect of this unique skyscraper – there is nothing quite like it anywhere else in the world – was William Pereira of Los Angeles. The building is topped by a 200ft/61m-high hollow spire, illuminated from within, its sides clad in aluminium sheeting.

Opening times
Viewing chamber
Mon.–Fri.
9am–4.30pm

There are 6000 windows in all and a viewing platform on the 27th floor (open: daily 8am–4pm).

On the east side of the Pyramid, on Clay Street, is a small park planted with 80 of the famous Californian redwood trees (see Muir Woods). The park is open to the public during normal business hours.

◀ *New symbol of San Francisco – the Transamerica Pyramid*

The nearby Bank Exchange Saloon stands on a site formerly occupied by the Montgomery Block, demolished in 1959. When erected 106 years earlier it was the first major building complex in San Francisco.

★Twin Peaks   F 12

MUNI station
Lines K, L, and M
to Castro Street,
then change to
bus no. 37
("Burnett")

Bus
37

Although rising 900ft/274m above sea level, Twin Peaks – the more southerly of the two is just 6ft/2m taller than its neighbour – is not the highest of San Francisco's 43 hills; that distinction belongs to Mount Davidson (by some 30ft/9m). Twin Peaks is however easier to reach and offers perhaps the finest views over the city and the bay.

For those with a car there is an easy route to the summit by road. Anyone using public transport faces a short but nevertheless quite steep walk up the final footpath (take the No. 37 bus up to Parkridge and Crestline from where the driver will point the way). Even in warm weather strong, cool winds often blow in off the Pacific late in the afternoon, so suitable extra clothing is recommended.

The summit is the only one in San Francisco still in something like a natural state, being neither built upon nor even laid out as gardens. There is nowhere better from which to view the city and the bay and take in the true scale of San Francisco. The Spanish called the twin peaks "Los pechos de la chola", i.e. the breasts of the Indian Maiden.

Union Square   I 9 (I 5)

Location
Geary Street and
Powell Street

San Francisco has no real centre, but Union Square comes closest to satisfying that description. Here or hereabouts various lines of communication converge; here too are found the best shops (Macy's, Magnin,

View from the Twin Peaks down over the city and bay of San Francisco

Neiman-Marcus, Saks Fifth Avenue) and the best hotels (Grand Hyatt San Francisco, Westin St Francis, Sir Francis Drake). A short step away, in Geary Street, stand San Francisco's leading theatres, and the south-west corner of the square itself, where Geary and Powell Streets meet, has the reputation of being the liveliest spot in the city. Three blocks south, in Market Street (see entry), stand the Cable Car Museum (see entry) and the Visitor Information Center.

Cable car
59

The site of Union Square was a gift to the city made by John M. Geary, the first American mayor. Its ornamental palm trees are unique in San Francisco. Ever since 1942 there has been a vast underground car park beneath the square. The name Union Square dates from the time of the American Civil War (1861–65) when mass demonstrations took place in support of the Northern Union and against the secessionist Southern States.

In 1902 a granite Corinthian column topped by a bronze goddess of victory was erected in the square to commemorate Admiral George Dewey's success against the Spanish fleet in the Bay of Manila during the short Spanish-American War of 1898.

Political demonstrations are still held in Union Square. But especially when the weather is warm its benches are a welcome refuge throughout the day for strollers and the poor from the slums south of Market Street (see entry).

Vedanta Temple

G 8

Situated in Cow Hollow (see entry) the Vedanta Temple is surely the most unusual building in the city. Erected in 1905 it was designed by the architect Joseph A. Leonard in collaboration with Swami Trigunatitananda who, five years earlier, had founded the Vedanta Society of North California, which is

Location
2963 Webster St., corner of Filbert St.

Union Square – centre point of a city that really has no centre

The city's two faces – skyscrapers and "Victorian" houses

Bus
41

still in existence. In its all but grotesque mixture of architectural styles – Queen Anne, Colonial, Oriental, Moorish and medieval – the temple is said to symbolise the Vedic doctrine that all religions are but different ways of approaching the one God. The Vedanta is the highest of the six systems of Hindu religious philosophy.

Note in particular the crenellated European castle tower on one side and the octagonal cupola such as is raised above a Shiva temple on the other. Between them is a double dome of the kind seen on Bengali temples.

★Victorian Houses

History

The architectural face of San Francisco is characterised on the one hand by the skyscrapers (see entry) of the city centre and on the other by the wooden houses of the residential suburbs. The latter, dating mainly from the 19th c., are on that account generally referred to as "Victorian". The city's swift development – from a mere village in 1850 to a town of 150,000 inhabitants 20 years later and a city of more than 300,000 at the turn of the century – demanded an economical way of building.

Although the very finest Victorian houses, built between 1870 and 1906, were destroyed in the earthquake (in particular those on Nob Hill and Van Ness Avenue), more than 13,000 still survive in various parts of the city – Bernal Heights, Duboce Triangle, Eureka, Glen Park, Haight-Ashbury, Mission District, Noe Valley, Potrero Hill and Western Addition.

Roughly half of them have undergone alteration, with new façades of asbestos sheeting, plaster and stone.

Italian style

Between 1870 and 1880 narrow-fronted houses were built in what became known as the Italian style on account of the arches and other Roman elements on the façades.

This Italian style developed in the 1880s into the distinctive San Francisco (as opposed to the simpler East Coast and Mid West) "Stick", so called because of the strong vertical emphasis of both the overall structure and the ornamentation, "like so many sticks". The term was first coined by the American architect Vincent Scully, though only after the houses had been built. Stick houses too have arches on their façades, the latter often being crowned by a gable and simple dormer window. The practice of painting the houses in pastel shades, recently revived for some restored houses, also dates from this time.

San Francisco "Stick"

In the 1890s the Queen Anne style came into favour, especially for the more expensive, detached type of house (with conical-roofed towers, loft gables and mass-produced ornamentation).
    In the construction of all these houses extensive use was made of the redwood readily available near San Francisco. It was durable and reasonably resistant to fire and insect damage.

Queen Anne style

Some particularly fine examples of Victorian houses can be seen in the area centred on the western half of Union Street, roughly from Gough Street to Divisadero Street (and Cow Hollow – see entry). There are also some very attractive houses around Alamo Square. This however is not a safe district for tourists to venture into on foot and care should be taken even if driving.

Where to see Victorian houses

San Francisco has only a few so-called cast-iron houses, recognisable by the iron stanchions inside and out on every floor. Perhaps the best-known of these buildings in San Francisco is Columbus Tower (920 Kearny Street, on the corner of Columbus Avenue). Dating from 1907, it is painted green and stands out from among the surrounding buildings all of which are low. Nowadays people like to photograph it with the Transamerica Pyramid (see entry) in the background; the contrast in styles is striking.

Cast-iron houses

War Memorial Opera House

See Civic Center

★Wells Fargo History Room
I 8 (J 5)

The Wells Fargo Bank building (main entrance in Montgomery Street), erected in 1959, is not itself of any great interest. But its museum is a rich source of information about the early history of California.
    One of the prize exhibits is a particularly fine example of a Concord coach, the name being taken from the town of Concord in New Hampshire where coaches of this type were built. When the Wells Fargo Express Co. was founded in San Francisco in 1852 by Henry Wells from Vermont and William Fargo from New York, Concord coaches were used to transport passengers and freight, especially gold. There are relics of the Gold Rush and exhibitions recalling the hard life of the "Forty-Niners".
    A special display is devoted to Black Bart. Over a period of just eight years, from about 1877 to 1885, he ambushed single-handed 28 coaches. He would frequently leave comic verses at the scene of the crime in which he claimed to be a sort of Robin Hood robbing the rich to give to the poor.
    There is a comprehensive library open to anybody who is interested.

Location
420 Montgomery Street

Opening times
Mon.–Fri.
9am–5pm

Entry free

World of Oil (Oil Museum)
I 8 (J 5)

This museum in the Standard Oil Company of California building will fascinate anybody interested in the story of oil, from its discovery to the development of the countless oil-based products.

Location
555 Market Street

Opening times
Mon.–Fri.
9am–4pm

The information is presented with exemplary clarity aided by models of equipment used in the oil-fields and three dioramas. There is also an eighteen minute multi-media show called "Magic of a Refinery". Screened several times each day it calls for no fewer than 26 projectors.

★★Yosemite National Park

Location
200 miles/320km east of San Francisco (via Highway 120 from north-west or 140 from south-west)

Yosemite (pronounced Yossémmitty) is the second oldest National Park in the United States (after Yellowstone). Despite the distance it is definitely worth visiting – what after all is 200 miles/320km when compared with the many thousands already travelled in reaching San Francisco? In theory the National Park is only a lengthy day trip from San Francisco by car or bus; but this really does impose a strain, and to become at all familiar with Yosemite takes at least three days.

Practical information

It is essential to book hotel accommodation in advance whatever the time of year, but particularly in the period from June to September when the tourist season is at its height. Most bookings for accommodation within the Park (Ahwahnee Hotel, Wawona Hotel, Yosemite Lodge, Curry Village) are handled by Central Reservations Yosemite Park, 5410 East Home, Fresno, CA 93727; tel. 209–252–4848.

Facilities in Yosemite Village include not only the hotels already mentioned, all of which have restaurants, but also shopping of every sort. All the information anyone might conceivably want relating to the Park is available at the Visitor Center (P.O.B. 557, Yosemite National Park, CA 95389; tel. 209–372–0200). The Visitor Center also issues the permits required by anyone intending to make use of one of the Park's six camp sites (tel. 900–454–2100).

There are several hundred miles of trails running through the Park, making for some magnificent walking. But it is essential to carry sufficient

One of nature's marvels – the Half Dome in Yosemite National Park

supplies; there are no services of any kind in the backcountry beyond the Valley.

History

The Yosemite region of the Sierra Nevada, covering an area of more than 888sq.miles/2300sq.km, was declared a US National Park in 1890, having been made a California State Park as early as 1864, during the American Civil War. White men first discovered the Yosemite Valley, amounting to only about 6sq.miles/15sq.km of the present Park, in 1851 when State troopers penetrated into the Valley in pursuit of Indians (there had been several attacks on white men panning gold in the foothills). The Indians escaped but the troopers reported back on the breathtaking beauty of the Yosemite Valley (the name comes from the Indian word "u-zu-ma-ta" referring to the grey bears found in the area).

In 1855 the first expedition on horseback entered the Valley along Indian trails. Others followed soon afterwards. To prevent private interests from spoiling the Valley, Congress passed a law obliging the new State of California to protect Yosemite and the groves of redwood (see Muir Park) at Mariposa. A decade later the first roads into the Valley were constructed. As early as 1877 coach journeys through it were being organised. In 1880 the Federal authorities assumed responsibility for the area, gradually extending the boundaries of the Park until it reached its present size. In 1900 the first automobile ventured into the Yosemite Valley and in 1907 a railroad was built as far as El Portal on the western boundary of the Park. It survived until 1945. In 1926 the all-weather Merced highway was completed; it is still the most popular route.

Brief description

It is of course impossible to describe here in any detail the many beauties of this magnificent National Park. The Yosemite Valley itself, through which the Merced River flows, is situated at an altitude of about 4266ft/1300m. Massive blocks of granite rise a further 4600ft/1400m in places. Towering some 3000ft/900m above the Valley floor is El Capitan (7571ft/2307m), in the vast bulk of which no fissure has yet been found.

Other impressive peaks include, on the opposite side of the Valley, the Three Brothers, Sentinel Rock and the two Cathedral Rocks first scaled only 50 or so years ago; also, further up the Valley, Eagle Peak (8500ft/2590m) and the Half Dome (8845ft/2695m). This monolith closing off the eastern end of the Valley is shaped like a dome split vertically down the middle; whether the other half ever existed remains unclear. The peaks best known to climbers are El Capitan and the Half Dome; these were among the first climbs to extend the scale of difficulty beyond grade 6. Some of these peaks come into view on emerging from the Wawona Tunnel.

The famous Yosemite Falls, approximately half way up the Valley, plunge 2425ft/739m in three stages. They are generally dry however from the end of June to the begining of November. The other waterfalls, such as the Bridal Veil Falls, are also reduced to mere trickles in the summer months.

Mariposa Grove, the most accessible of the Park's three redwood groves (the other two are Tuolumne Grove and Merced Grove, deep in the backcountry) lies about 2 miles/3km from the South Entrance. Anyone who has already visited Muir Woods (see entry) will immediately spot the difference between the two species of redwood. *Sequoia sempervirens* in Muir Woods reaches a greater height but is smaller in circumference than *Sequoia giganteum* which grows in the Yosemite Park and is one of the world's largest plants.

Mariposa Grove boasts about 500 of these enormous trees. The largest, which stands in the lower part of the grove, is known as Giant Grizzly; despite having lost its crown – broken off under the weight of snow – it still stands 230ft/70m tall. The diameter of the trunk at its base measures 30ft/9m while some of the boughs branching off at a height of 90ft/27m are 6½ft/2m thick. This tree is estimated to be 2700 years old.

Not far from the Tioga road (the road into the park from the north-east, open only in the summer months) there are several very beautiful mountain lakes. The loveliest is May Lake at an altitude of 8200ft/2500m. Equally worth while is an excursion to Glacier Point (7220ft/2200m) from where there are breathtaking views of the other peaks in the Yosemite Valley.

It has been accurately established that 76 species of mammals live in the park, including the dangerous grey bear and the brown bear: respect the warning notices! There are also 221 species of birds, 29 species of reptiles, 37 species of trees and hundreds of different sorts of flowers and plants.

Zoo

See San Francisco Zoological Gardens

Lombard Street – zigzags and hydrangeas ▶

Practical Information

Accommodation

See Hotels, Youth hostels

Airport

Location

San Francisco International Airport is situated about 14 miles/22.5km south of downtown San Francisco.

Getting to downtown San Francisco

Passengers can take taxis, Airporter buses or use the hotel limousine services.

By taxi

The taxi fare is about $25 plus tip.

By Airporter bus

Airporter buses connect the airport and the Airline Terminal downtown. They depart from in front of the airport's Central and South Terminals directly by the baggage checkout. Frequency: 6am–10pm, every 15 minutes; 10pm–midnight, every half hour; midnight–6am, depending on incoming flights. The transfer from the airport to the downtown Air Terminal costs $7 ($11 return) and takes between 20 and 30 minutes.

Air Terminal

The Air Terminal is located on the corner of Taylor Street and Ellis Street in the centre of San Francisco, at the heart of the hotel district. For times of arrival and departure of buses linking the airport and Air Terminal dial 673–2433.

Limousines

There are also limousines which will take passengers to the hotels.

Banks

See Currency

BART (rapid rail system)

See Public transportation

Beaches

Although San Francisco is almost totally surrounded by water, the sea temperature is seldom high enough for beaches to offer comfortable bathing. What sandy beaches there are, e.g. in Aquatic Park and the Golden Gate National Recreation Area, tend to be used chiefly for sunbathing, with only a hardy few venturing in the water. Even in August the sea temperature rarely exceeds 59°F/15°C.

For a swim in the ocean San Franciscans have to travel almost 70 miles/110km south to Santa Cruz; even there the season for bathing is fairly short. There are some good beaches further south still at Carmel (Pebble Beach, north of Carmel; Carmel River State Beach to the south).

Bakers Beach and the Golden Gate Bridge

Boat Tours

Blue and Gold Fleet, tel. 781–7877. Trips of about 1¼hrs in San Francisco Bay. Frequent departures from Pier 39 (West Marina) from 10am.

Hornblower Yachts, tel. 394–8900. Daily from Pier 33: 3-hour dinner cruise, dep. 7.30pm; Fridays only: 2-hour lunch cruise, dep. 11.30am; Sundays: 2½-hour brunch cruise in the Bay, dep. 10.30am. All cruises aboard the 164ft/50m "City of San Francisco" (three decks).

Red and White Fleet, tel. 546–2896. Frequent trips every day from Fisherman's Wharf (Pier 41), 10.45am onwards; ¾-hour trips in the Bay; also to Sausalito, Tiburon, Alcatraz and Angel Island.

Bookshops

A Clean Well-lighted Place for Books
601 Van Ness Avenue

Books Inc.
140 Powell Street
San Francisco's oldest bookshop, established in 1851.

City Lights
261 Columbus Avenue
Founded and run by the poet Lawrence Ferlinghetti
(see Famous People)

Dalton
200 Kearny Street and 2 Embarcadero Center

Breakdown Assistance

Doubleday
265 Sutter Street

Inc. Donald's
49 Turk Street

Sierra Club
730 Polk Street

Waldenbooks
Embarcadero Center

Breakdown Assistance

Vehicle
recovery

N.B. The cost of having a car towed away can be very high.

If you have a breakdown in a rented car (see Rent-a-car), inform the rental company immediately and follow their instructions/advice.

If the car is not rented, call the California State Automobile Association, American Automobile Association (AAA) or similar organisation; these offer a free repair and breakdown recovery service to members.

If the car is still capable of being driven, refer to the "Automobile Repairing Service" section in "Yellow Pages" for the nearest garage.

Foreign makes
of car

Visitors bringing in cars not engineered to US standards should ensure beforehand that the vehicle is in good working order. While most big cities are likely to have a dealer capable of repairing foreign makes of car (consult "Automobile Repairing Service" in "Yellow Pages"), spare parts may not be readily available.

Automobile
Associations

California State Automobile Association, 150 Van Ness Avenue, San Francisco, CA 94102, tel. 565–2012

American Automobile Association (AAA), tel. 1–800–336–HELP (national emergency number)

Buses

See Rail and bus services, Public transportation

Business Hours

Chemists

See Drugstores

Banks

See Currency

Shops

Business hours are not controlled by law, so shops and restaurants stay open as long as they please. Quite a few shops, supermarkets included, remain open round the clock, seven days a week, closing on public holidays only (Thanksgiving Day and Christmas Day in particular).

Principal
shopping areas

In the principal shopping areas (Union Square, Jackson Square, Sutter Street) many of the shops close at about 6.30pm; some however stay open until 9pm or even later.

Some shops outside these areas have adopted similar hours but it is quite common to find small delicatessens, etc. open until midnight or beyond.

In high season almost all the shops in the shopping centres around Fisherman's Wharf (Ghirardelli Square, The Cannery, The Anchorage, Pier 39) stay open until 9 or 10pm; out of season they shut at 8.30pm.

See entries for particular museums in the A to Z section, also Practical Information, Museums. Museums

See Postal services Post offices

Restaurants generally stay open until midnight or 1am. Most of the eating places in the Zim chain are open round the clock. Restaurants

Cable cars

See Public transportation

Camping

There is an RV Park for motor caravans in King Street, close to central San Francisco. While not particularly attractive the concreted Park is conveniently situated, being within walking distance of many downtown sights and with a good bus service into the city centre.

Car hire

See Rent-a-car

Chemists

See Drugstores

Churches

Only a handful of San Francisco's churches survived the 1906 earthquake; most of those erected since 1906 are traditional in style and often modelled on ecclesiastical buildings abroad.

For descriptions of St Mary's Cathedral, Grace Cathedral, Old St Mary (Chinatown) and Mission Dolores, see the A to Z section. Among the most interesting of San Francisco's other churches are:

First Baptist Church of San Francisco (1910), Market Street/Octavia Street
First Unitarian Church (1889), 1187 Franklin Street
Glide Memorial United Methodist Church
Holy Trinity Russian Orthodox Cathedral (1909), 1520 Green Street
Notre-Dame des Victoires (Cath., 1913), 566 Bush Street
Old First Presbyterian Church (1911), Van Ness Avenue and Sacramento Street
Russian Holy Virgin Cathedral of the Church in Exile (1961), 6210 Geary Boulevard
St Boniface Church (Cath., 1908), 133 Golden Gate Avenue
St Francis of Assisi (Cath., 1849), 610 Vallejo Street
St Luke's Episcopal Church (1910), Van Ness Avenue and Clay Street
St Mark's Evangelical Lutheran Church (1895), 1111 O'Farrell Street
St Matthew's Lutheran Church, 3281 16th Street, corner of Dolores
St Peter and St Paul Church (Cath., 1924), 666 Filbert Street
Trinity Episcopal Church (1892), 1668 Bush Street

Temple Emanu-El (1927), Arguello Boulevard and Lake Street Synagogue

Church of St Peter and St Paul (see page 129)

Cinemas

Première cinemas
There are surprisingly few première cinemas in downtown San Francisco; all of them are in Market Street:

Egyptian, Market Street and Sixth Street, tel. 673–7373
Embassy, Market Street and Seventh Street, tel. 431–5221
St Francis I & II, Market Street between Fifth and Sixth Street, tel. 362–4822
Strand, Market Street between Seventh and Eighth Street, tel. 621–2227.

Film festival
San Francisco's highly prestigious international film festival held in late April/early May is the oldest such festival in the USA. It takes place in the Palace of Fine Arts and Castro Theatre (corner of Market Street and Castro Streets). Several top film-makers live in San Francisco.

"San Francisco Experience"
The "San Francisco Experience" at Pier 39 (daily, every half hour, 11am–11pm) offers a unique and totally absorbing form of entertainment. Numerous projectors create an extraordinary sense of realism as the audience relives historic and other notable events, such as the 1906 earthquake, Haight-Ashbury in the heyday of the Flower People and the Chinese New Year celebrations in San Francisco's Chinatown.

San Francisco on screen
San Francisco itself has "starred" in more films than any other American city apart from New York. Its popularity with Hollywood is borne out by a long list of titles including "Hello Frisco" (1924), "In Old San Francisco" (1927), "San Francisco Nights" (1928), "Frisco Jenny" (1933), "San Francisco" (1936), "San Francisco Docks" (1940), "Hello, Frisco, Hello" (1943), "Man from Frisco" (1944), "San Francisco Story" (1952), "Incident in San Francisco" (1971) and "Slaughter in San Francisco" (1973), not forgetting the television series "The Streets of San Francisco".

Consulates

See Diplomatic and consular offices

Credit cards

See Currency

Crime

San Francisco has its share of crime just like any other big city. Extreme care is needed entering some parts of the city, while others are best avoided altogether. That said, San Francisco is unquestionably one of the loveliest cities in the world and by taking a few elementary precautions enjoyment of it need not be marred. Cars should whenever possible be parked overnight in an underground garage. If leaving the car unattended during the day, lock all possessions in the boot. Do not visit parks after dark.

The Western Addition–Hayes Valley area bounded by Hayes Street (south), Geary Street (north), Gough Street (east) and Steiner Street (west) has the worst reputation for attacks on tourists. Avoid walking through the area e.g. on the way from City Hall to Golden Gate Park, even if it looks the obvious route according to the map.

No-go areas

Nor should tourists attempt to take photographs around Alamo Square, e.g. of the Victorian houses with the Transamerica Pyramid in the background (such an action is likely to result in a police caution if nothing else).

Currency

The basic US unit of currency is the dollar ($1) equal to 100 cents. Coins are minted in 1 cent (penny), 5 cents (nickel), 10 cents (dime), 25 cents (quarter), 50 cents (half dollar, less common) and 1 dollar. Banknotes (referred to as bills) in general circulation are in denominations of $1, $2, $5, $10, $20, $50 and $100. Notes of higher denomination are also available from banks within the United States.

US American banknotes of all denominations are identical in size and colour. They are distinguished one from another only by the value printed on them and the pictures on each side (black obverse, green reverse).

N.B.

There are no restrictions on the amount of money that can be brought into or taken out of the United States. Cash or monetary instruments to a value of $10,000 or more must however be declared on the customs declaration form.

Currency regulations

Dollar rates of exchange and commission charges are generally less favourable within the USA than in Europe. So it is advisable to purchase US dollars before departure and to take a sufficient quantity of small change (notes of $1 to $10) for immediate use.

Exchanging foreign currency

Shops and restaurants will not accept any foreign currency whatsoever; some banks will, but their charges are high.

Since changing foreign currency in the USA is often difficult (no exchange facilities in hotels; time-consuming checks at banks) and there is generally a sizeable cost involved, it is best to purchase US dollars in Europe. Travellers' cheques (low rate of commission) obtained from the visitor's own

Travellers' cheques

bank or from a European branch of American Express offer the best security. Eurocheques are not suitable for the USA.

If American Express cheques are lost or stolen they will usually be replaced by the nearest American Express branch on presentation of the sales advice note issued when the cheques were purchased.

Credit cards

Credit cards are a widely accepted form of payment and often better than a passport as proof of identity. For renting a car a credit card is essential. Filling stations on the other hand only accept cash.

The most widely used credit cards are Mastercard and Visa. Most restaurants and shops will take American Express but only a few accept Diner's Club.

The credit cards issued by some companies enabling the holder (with a PIN number) to draw money from cash machines in banks and supermarkets can be extremely useful in the US.

Banks

Banks are generally open for normal business Mon.–Fri. 9am–6pm. Many however will not exchange foreign currency. In San Francisco there are bureaux de change at:

Bank of America
345 Montgomery Street, tel. 622–2451
Open: Mon.–Thur. 9am–3pm, Fri. until 5pm

Bank of America
Powell and Market Street, tel. 622–4098
Open: Mon.–Thur. 10am–3pm, Fri. until 5pm

Thomas Cook Currency Services
100 Grant Street, tel. 362–3452
Open: Mon.–Fri. 9am–5pm, Sat. 10am–2pm

Foreign Exchange LTD
415 Stockton Street, tel. 397–4700
Open: Mon.–Fri. 8.30am–5pm, Sat. 9am–1.30pm

Bureaux de change at the airport

The South Terminal at San Francisco International Airport, where the vast majority of travellers arrive and depart, has two bureaux de change:

Bank of America (International Building)
Open: daily 7am–11pm

Thomas Cook Currency Services (Departure Level)
Open: daily 7.30am–11pm

Customs Regulations

Visitors arriving in the United States must fill in a customs declaration and an immigration form. The necessary forms will normally be issued on the aircraft.

Personal effects (clothing, toilet articles, jewellery, cameras and cine cameras, films, binoculars, portable typewriters, radios, tape-recorders and television sets, sports equipment, etc.) may be taken into the United States without payment of duty. In addition there are duty-free allowances for adults of 1 quart of alcoholic liquor and 300 cigarettes or 50 cigars or 3 pounds of tobacco. Gifts to the value of 100 dollars per head (including, for adults, up to 1 gallon of alchoholic liquor and 100 cigars) may also be taken in duty-free; any such items are required to be available for inspection by customs so should not be gift-wrapped.

Special regulations govern the import of animals, meat and plants. Information about these can be obtained from the US customs authorities.

Department stores

See Shopping

Doctors

See Medical assistance, Emergencies

Diplomatic and Consular Offices

United States Embassies and Consulates

Embassy: United Kingdom
24–31 Grosvenor Square
London W1A 1AE
Tel. (0171) 499 9000

Consulates:
3 Regent Terrace
Edinburgh EH7 5BW
Tel. (0131) 556 8315

Queen's House
14 Queen Street, Belfast BT1 6EQ
Tel. (01232) 328239

Embassy: Ireland
42 Elgin Road, Ballsbridge, Dublin
Tel. (01) 687122

Embassy: Canada
100 Wellington Street
Ottawa, Ontario K1P 5T1
Tel. (613) 238 5335

Consulates in Calgary, Halifax, Montreal, Québec City, Toronto and
Vancouver

Embassy: Australia
Moonah Place
Canberra, ACT 2600
Tel. (062) 270 5000

Consulates in Brisbane, Melbourne, Perth and Sydney

Embassy: New Zealand
29 Fitzherbert Terrace, Thorndon
Wellington
Tel. (04) 722068

Consulate in Auckland

Foreign Embassies and Consulates in the United States/San Francisco

Embassy: United Kingdom
3100 Massachusetts Avenue NW
Washington, DC 20008
Tel. (202) 462 1340

Consulate-General:
1 Sansome Street, Suite 850
San Francisco, CA 94104
Tel. (415) 981 3030

Ireland

Embassy:
2234 Massachusetts Avenue NW
Washington, DC 20008
Tel. (202) 462 3939

Canada

Embassy:
501 Pennsylvania Avenue NW
Washington, DC 20001
Tel. (202) 682 1740

Drugstores

American drugstores or pharmacies are not at all like European chemists shops. Most are more like a general store and also sell food and drink. In the majority of cases dispensing medicines on prescription forms only a small part of their business.

Medicines not requiring a prescription are also obtainable in most supermarkets, many of which stay open round the clock.

Information

Drugstores are listed in "Yellow Pages", copies of which are found in most hotel rooms.

Opening times

Usually 9am to 6pm; some stay open until 9pm or even midnight.

Emergency
service

Drugstores do not operate a night emergency service. In an emergency go to the nearest hospital (all of which have their own pharmacies).

Electricity

110 volts AC. Any electric razors, hair-driers, irons, etc. not of the dual-voltage type require a voltage transformer (otherwise just an adapter plug).

Suitable transformers and adapters are best obtained before setting out for the United States although, if necessary, they can be bought in the US at a hardware or department store.

Emergencies

Emergency calls

For ambulance, police or fire department dial 911.

Emergency
hospital

Dial 413–2800 or 821–8111

Breakdown
assistance

See entry.

Events

End of January
–mid February.

Chinese New Year celebrations in Chinatown (Information: Chinese Chamber of Commerce, 730 Sacramento Street, tel. 982–3000)

International Film Festival (see Cinemas)	End of March
Easter Sunday Sunrise Festival, Mount Davidson	—mid April
Cherry Blossom Festival in the Japan Center, Post and Geary Streets: Japanese music, dancing, films, tea ceremony, Bonsai demonstrations, calligraphy, etc. (Information: tel. 986–6140)	2nd half of April
Latin-American Fiesta and Parade (in Mission)	May
Cable Car Festival	June
Lesbian-Gay Parade	
Independence Day Fireworks on the Crissy Field near the marina	July
Nihonmachi Street Festival in Japantown (street party, Japanese music)	August
Outdoor art exhibition in Civic Center Plaza	September
Japanese autumn festival (Aki Matsuri) in the Japan Center (Information: tel. 346–3242 or 922–6776)	
Columbus Day (Monday preceding October 12th)	October
Columbus Festival at North Beach and Fisherman's Wharf with grand procession	
End of October: Rodeo, horse and cattle show in the Cow Palace, Geneva Avenue (tel. 334–4852)	

Excursions

See Sightseeing tours

Ferries

See Public transportation

Food and Drink

Even without the time or money for a meal in a restaurant (see entry), no one need ever go hungry in San Francisco; there is almost always a fast food outlet somewhere near offering typical American hamburgers, hot dogs or pizzas.

Hot dogs are frankfurters in a split roll, served with mustard and sauerkraut. Pizza pies are Italian-style pizzas eaten hot. Hamburgers need no introduction. Coffee shops, drugstores and lunch counters sell the most popular fast food of all: a corned beef, roast beef or pastrami and rye bread sandwich, with a gherkin and a cup of coffee.

Fast food

The usual American drink at breakfast or other meals is a lightly roasted, thin coffee or caffeine-free coffee ("sanka" or "postum"). A second cup of coffee (or tea, made with a tea-bag) is often provided at no further charge. Drinking chocolate and soft drinks such as cola, tonic, fruit juices, sodas, club sodas (plain carbonated water), milk and milk shakes are available everywhere and are usually served "iced" unless otherwise ordered. Root beer is another drink widely available in drugstores and from vending machines. Originally it was made from the root and bark of the sassafras tree which, after fermentation, produced a mildly alcoholic drink. Nowadays it is manufactured from water, sugar, a dark colouring agent and various spices; no longer alcoholic it is something of an acquired taste.

Drinks

135

American beer, always served cold, is somewhat lighter than a typical European beer. It is served by the glass, stein, seidel, schooner or pitcher. Many of the breweries were founded by German immigrants. The most common brands are Budweiser, Schlitz, Falstaff, Pabst Busch, Lone Star, Coors, La Crosse and Miller. Imported beers (many from Germany) are popular but expensive.

Before a meal it is usual to have a cocktail, often fancifully named and with a whiskey, gin, vodka, vermouth or rum base. The favourite spirits (liquors) are whiskey, (Bourbon, Scotch, Canadian, Rye, Irish or blended), vodka, gin, rum, brandy, vermouth and liqueurs ("cordial").

In restaurants water, generally ice cold, is provided free with meals.

Galleries

Most of San Francisco's galleries are located downtown in and around Sutter Street. Almost all have permanent exhibitions and most of them are open either Mon.–Sat. or Tue.–Sun., 10am–5pm or 6pm. Those listed below are among the better known:

Allrich Gallery, 251 Post Street, tel 398–8896
Atelier Dore, Inc., 771 Bush Street, tel. 391–2423
Braunstein Quay Gallery, 245 Sutter Street, tel. 392–5532
Fraenkel Gallery, 55 Grant Avenue, tel. 981–2661
Gump's Gallery, 250 Post Street, tel. 982–1616
Hanson Galleries, 153 Maiden Lane, tel. 956–4338
Harcourts Gallery, 460 Bush Street, tel. 421–3428
John Berggruen Gallery, 228 Grant Avenue, tel. 781–4629
John Pence Gallery, 750 Post Street, tel. 441–1138
Kabutoya Galleries, 454 Sutter Street, tel. 434–2777
Kertesz Fine Art Gallery, 521 Sutter Street, tel. 626–0376
Maxwell Galleries, 551 Sutter Street, tel. 421–5193
Pascal de Sarthe Gallery, 315 Sutter Street, tel. 397–0168
Pasquale Iannetti Art Gallery, 522 Sutter Street, tel. 433–2771
Richard Thompson Gallery, 80 Maiden Lane, tel. 956–2114
San Francisco Art Exchange, 458 Geary Street, tel. 441–8840
San Francisco Gallery, 41 Powell Street, tel. 434–8745
Stephen Wirtz Gallery, 49 Geary Street, tel. 433–6879
Vorpal Gallery, 393 Grove Street, tel. 397–2200

Getting to San Francisco

Although for some foreign visitors San Francisco is a port of call on a cruise, and others come by campervan, the vast majority arrive by air. San Francisco International Airport (see Airport), situated about 15½ miles/25km south of the city centre, handles international and domestic USA flights.

Flights from Europe to the USA

There are numerous scheduled flights from London and other European airports, many of which fly non-stop to major American cities including San Francisco (British Airways, Virgin Atlantic). There are also frequent charter flights, principally during the main holiday season and to the popular holiday destinations.

Special rates

Some American Airlines (e.g. USAir, American Airlines, Continental, Delta) offer combined air tickets at advantageous rates, covering the transatlantic crossing and onward flights to US cities such as San Francisco.

Small change

Anyone flying direct from Europe should be sure to have plenty of small change – US coins, $1 and $5 notes – for cab fares, phone calls, tips, etc.

Proffering large denomination bank notes can cause difficulty and incurs the risk of fraud.

Help for the Disabled

Building regulations in the USA vary considerably from state to state. In recent years the authorities have been concerned to ensure that public buildings, airports, railroad stations, hotels, restaurants, etc., have proper facilities for disabled people. Theme parks and other places of entertainment also try to make special provision; parking lots allocated specifically for disabled drivers are almost universal.

In Britain the main sources of information and advice on travel by the disabled are the Royal Association for Disability and Rehabilitation (RADAR), 25 Mortimer Street, London W1N 8AB, tel. (0171) 637 5400; the Spinal Injuries Association, 76 St James's Lane, London N10 3DF, tel. (0181) 444 2121; and Mobility International, 62 Union Street, London SE1, tel. (0171) 403 5688.

Information in the UK

"Holiday and Travel Abroad – A Guide for Disabled People", published by RADAR.

Useful publications

"The World Wheelchair Traveller", published by the AA for the Spinal Injuries Association.

"Low Cost Travel Tips for People Using Wheelchairs", published by Mobility International.

The AA also publishes a "Guide for the Disabled Traveller" (free to members).

Hotels

San Francisco now has more hotel rooms than any comparable city of its size, the many new luxury hotels built in recent years having increased the number of rooms to almost 30,000. While this is sufficient to meet normal demand, when the city is hosting one or more conventions beds can still be in short supply. So anyone planning to arrive in San Francisco in the evening is well advised to book accommodation in advance. Among the very newest hotels, built in the last two years, are the Park Hyatt, the Ritz Carlton and the completely renovated Sheraton Palace.

Almost without exception the hotels listed below offer rooms with en suite bathroom, air conditioning and colour TV.

In contrast to Europe, breakfast is never included in the room charge; indeed many smaller US hotels do not serve breakfast at all. Even when they do, guests are under no obligation to breakfast in the hotel and will always find what they want at a nearby diner, lunch counter, etc.

Breakfast

Most hotels, especially the larger ones, have one or more restaurants; prices vary according to the category of hotel.

Hotel restaurants

All hotels have safes in which cash, jewellery or other valuables can be deposited. Room keys are not usually handed in to reception until final checkout.

Safes
Hotel keys

No charge is made for children occupying the same room as parents; additional adults however incur a charge of $10 to $20. Sales tax of 6.5%

Prices and payment

137

and Occupancy Tax (10% or more of the room charge) must be added to the bill. Accounts are best settled by travellers' cheque or credit card.

Anyone visiting more than a single destination can make significant savings by staying at hotels belonging to the same chain. Bookings should be made through a travel agent before departure.

Reservations

Advance booking is highly advisable. Many hotels have freephone numbers (prefix 1–800) and can be called up from anywhere in the USA free of charge.

Price categories

Luxury hotels (single room over $150, double room over $180)
High amenity hotels (single room $125–$150, double room $140–$180)
Good quality hotels (single room $90–$125, double room $100–$140)
Reasonably priced hotels (single room $70–$90, double room $80–$100)
Very reasonably priced hotels (single room about $50, double room about $60)

Luxury hotels

★ANA San Francisco (675 r.), 50 Third Street, tel. 974–6400/1–800–543–4300

★Campton Place Kempinski (126 r.), 340 Stockton Street, tel. 781–5555/1–800–426–3135

★Donatello (95 r.), 501 Post Street, tel. 441–7100/1–800–277–3184 (1–800–792–9837

★Fairmont Hotel and Tower (595 r.), 950 Mason Street, tel. 772–5000/1–800–527–4727

★Four Seasons Clift (329 r.), 495 Geary Street, tel. 775–4700/1–800–332–3442

★Huntington (143 r.), 1075 California Street, tel. 474–5400/1–800–227–4683

★Grand Hyatt San Francisco (693 r.), 345 Stockton Street, tel. 398–1234/1–800–233–1234

Entrance to the Mark Hopkins Hotel

★Hyatt Regency San Francisco (806 r.), 5 Embarcadero Center, tel. 788–1234/1–800–233–1234

★Mark Hopkins Inter-Continental (400 r.), 1 Nob Hill, tel. 392–3434/1–800–327–0200

★Nikko San Francisco (529 r.), Mason and O'Farrell Streets, tel. 394–1111/1–800–645–5687

★Pan Pacific Hotel San Francisco (348 r.), 500 Post Street, tel. 771–8600/1–800–553–6465

★Park Fifty Five Hotel (1004 r.), 55 Cyril Magnin Street, tel. 392–8000/1–800–338–1338

★Park Hyatt San Francisco (360 r.), 333 Battery, tel. 392–1234/1–800–228–9000

★Ritz Carlton San Francisco (336 r.), corner of California and Stockton Streets, tel. 296–7465/1–800–241–3333

★San Francisco Hilton (1907 r.), 333 O'Farrell Street, tel. 771–1400/1–800–445–8667

★San Francisco Marriott (1500 r.), Market & Fourth Streets, tel. 896–1600/1–800–228–9290

★Sheraton at Fisherman's Wharf (525 r.), 2500 Mason Street, tel. 362–5500/1–800–325–3535

★Sheraton Palace (550 r.), 2 New Montgomery Street, tel. 392–8600/1–800–325–3535

★Sherman House, 2160 Green Street

★Stouffer Stanford Court (402 r.), 905 California Street, tel. 989–3500/1–800–227–4726

★Westin St Francis (1200 r.), Union Square, tel. 397–2000/1–800–327–3608

Cathedral Hill (400 r.), Van Ness Avenue and Geary Street, tel. 776–8200/1–800–227–4730

Galleria Park (177 r.), 191 Sutter Street, tel. 781–3060/1–800–792–9639

High amenity hotels

San Francisco's Hyatt Regency Hotel in Embarcadero Center

Holiday Inn Financial District (557 r.), 750 Kearny Street, tel. 433–6600/
1–800–HOLIDAY

Holiday Inn Fisherman's Wharf (580 r.), 1300 Columbus Street, tel. 771–
9000/1–800–HOLIDAY

Holiday Inn Union Square (405 r.), 480 Sutter Street. tel. 398–8900/1–800–
HOLIDAY

Hyatt at Fisherman's Wharf (313 r.), 555 North Point, tel. 563–1234/1–800–
228–9000

San Francisco Airport Hilton (541 r.), San Francisco International Airport,
tel. 589–0770/1–800–445–8667

Sir Francis Drake (415 r.), 450 Powell Street, tel. 392–7755/1–800–227–5480

Tuscan Inn at Fisherman's Wharf (199 r.), 425 North Point, tel.
561–1100/1–800–648–4626

Good quality hotels

Bedford (150 r.), 761 Post Street, tel. 673–6040/1–800–227–5642

Bellevue (189 r.), 505 Geary Street, tel. 474–3600/1–800–421–8851

Holiday Inn Civic Center (390 r.), 50 Eighth Street, tel. 626–6103/1–800–
HOLIDAY

Holiday Inn Golden Gateway (497 r.), 1500 Van Ness Avenue, tel. 441–4000/
1–800–HOLIDAY

Howard Johnson's Motor Lodge (128 r.), 520 Beach Street, tel. 775–3800/
1–800–654–2000

Mansion Hotel, 2220 Sacramento Street

Miyako Hotel (208 r.), 1625 Post Street, tel. 922–3200/1–800–533–4567

Ramada Inn Fisherman's Wharf (231 r.), 590 Bay Street, tel. 885–4700/
1–800–228–2828

Raphael (150 r.), 386 Geary Street, tel. 986–2000/1–800–821–5343

Shannon Court, 550 Geary Street, tel. 775–5000/1–800–821–0493 (1–800–
228–8830 within California)

Washington Square Park, 1660 Stockton Street

Reasonably priced hotels

Beresford Arms, 701 Post Street, tel. 673–2600/1–800–533–6533

Best Western Americania Motor Lodge (145 r.), 121 Seventh Street, tel.
626–0200/1–800–227–4368

Best Western Canterbury/Whitehall (265 r.), 750 Sutter Street, tel. 474–
6464/1–800–227–4788

Best Western Civic Center Motor Inn (57 r.), 364 Ninth Street, tel. 621–2826/
1–800–444–5816

Best Western Grosvenor Airport Inn (206 r.), 380 South Airport Boulevard,
tel. 873–3200/1–800–528–1234

Best Western Kyoto Inn (125 r.), 1800 Sutter Street, tel. 921–4000/1–800–
528–1234

Californian (250 r.), 405 Taylor Street, tel. 885–2500/1–800–227–3346

Handlery Union Square Hotel (295 r.), 351 Geary Street, tel. 781–7800/
1–800–223–0888

Holiday Lodge (85 r.), 1901 Van Ness Avenue, tel. 776–4469

King George (144 r.), 334 Mason Street, tel. 781–5050/1–800–227–4240

Phoenix Inn, 601 Eddy Street, tel. 776–1380

Quality Hotel (145 r.), 2775 Van Ness Avenue, tel. 928–5000/1–800–221–
2222

San Francisco (499 r.), 1231 Market Street, tel. 626–8000/1–800–227–4747

Savoy (83 r.), 580 Geary Street, tel. 441–2700/1–800–227–4223

Villa Florence (177 r.), 225 Powell Street, tel. 397–7700/1–800–553–4411

Very reasonably priced hotels

Beresford (114 r.), 635 Sutter Street, tel. 673–9900/1–800–227–4048

Beresford Arms (102 r.), 701 Post Street, tel. 673–2600/1–800–533–6533

Carlton (165 r.), 1075 Sutter Street, tel. 673–0242/1–800–227–4496

Cartwright (121 r.), 524 Sutter Street, tel. 421–2865/1–800–227–3844

Chancellor (150 r.), 433 Powell Street, tel. 362–2004

Commodore International (113 r.), 825 Sutter Street, tel. 923–6800/1–800–
338–6848

El Cortez (170 r.), 550 Geary Street, tel. 775–5000/1–800–821–0493

Mark Twain (115 r.), 345 Taylor Street, tel. 673–2332/1–800–331–8349
Pickwick (192 r.), 85 Fifth Street, tel. 421–7500/1–800–227–3282
Triton (144 r.), 342 Grant Avenue, tel. 781–3566/1–800–227–3818

The Women's Hotel (14 r.), 642 Jones Street, tel. 775–1711 | Women-only hotel

A brochure "The Californias 1995 – Bed and Breakfast Inns" is obtainable from the California Department of Commerce, Office of Tourism, Dept. B & B, 801 K Street, Suite 1600, Sacramento, CA 95814. It lists 300 or so addresses in California offering bed and breakfast accommodation, with a short description of each. | Bed and Breakfast

Information

See Tourist information

Insurance

It is essential to take out short-term health and accident insurance when visiting the United States; the cost of medical treatment is high. Baggage insurance and, particularly in the case of a package holiday, insurance against cancellation, are also advisable. Arrangements can be made though a travel agent or insurance company; many tour operators now include insurance as part of their overall holiday package.

Visitors arriving in the United States can effect the necessary insurance through:

American International Underwriters,
1225 Connecticut Avenue, NW, Suite 414,
Washington D.C. 20036

UK address:
120 Fenchurch, London WC3M 5BP

Jazz

See Nightlife

Language

Differences abound between British and American usage. Some of the more commonly encountered are listed below:

British	*American*
appointment	date
attractive	cute
autumn	fall
bill	check
biscuit	cracker, cookie
bonnet (of car)	hood
boot (of car)	trunk
braces	suspenders
caravan	trailer

Language

British	American
chemist (shop)	drugstore
Christian name	first name
cinema	movies (movie theater)
cloakroom	checkroom
cupboard	closet
dustbin	garbage can
eiderdown	comforter
man	guy
first floor	second floor
flat	apartment
football	soccer
fortnight	two weeks
gangway	aisle
"gents" (lavatory)	men's room
glasses (spectacles)	eyeglasses
graduation (university, etc.)	commencement
ground floor	first floor
handbag	purse
label	sticker
holiday	vacation
"ladies" (lavatory)	ladies' room, powder room
lavatory	rest room
lavatory (roadside)	comfort station
lift	elevator
lorry	truck
luggage	baggage
maize	corn
nappy	diaper
town square	plaza
pavement	sidewalk
personal call (on telephone)	person to person call
petrol	gas, gasoline
policeman	cop
post	mail
post code	zip code
queue	(stand in) line
railway line, platform	track
refrigerator	icebox
repair	fix
return ticket	round trip ticket
reversed charge	collect (on telephone)
ring up, telephone	call
rubber	eraser
scone	biscuit
second floor	third floor
shop	store
single ticket	one-way ticket
spanner	wrench
subway	underpass
summer time	daylight saving time
surname	last name
sweets	candy
take-away	"to go" (in cafeteria, etc.)
tap	faucet
tin	can
tram	streetcar
trousers	pants
trunk call	long-distance call
undercut	tenderloin
underground	subway

British	American
viewpoint, viewing platform	observatory
Whitsun	Pentecost

N.B. It is worth re-iterating that in America the floors of buildings are always numbered starting at street level; thus "first floor" refers to what in Britain would be called the ground floor, "second floor" to what in Britain would be called the first floor, and so on.

Lost property

BART Lost and Found Bureau
Twelfth Street Station, City Center (Oakland), tel. 510–465–4100.
Open: Mon.–Fri. noon–6pm.

Medical Assistance

Doctors (physicians) and dentists are listed in "Yellow Pages"; hotel reception will also help locate them. Otherwise contact the hospital (see Emergencies).

Bills for doctors' services and medicines have to be settled immediately. Since no reciprocal agreement exists between the United States and the UK, medical insurance is essential. In the event of any claim arising, policy holders should contact their insurers as soon as possible.

Movies

See Cinemas

Museums

Asian Art Museum   Art museums
See A to Z, Golden Gate Park

California Palace of the Legion of Honor
See A to Z, California Palace of the Legion of Honor

San Francisco Museum of Modern Art
See A to Z, San Francisco Museum of Modern Art

M. H. de Young Memorial Museum
See A to Z, Golden Gate Park

Stanford University Museum of Art
See A to Z, Stanford University Museum of Art

University Art Museum. See A to Z, Berkeley

African-American Historical and Cultural Society   Other museums
See A to Z, San Francisco African-American Historical and Cultural Society

Believe it or not
See A to Z, Fisherman's Wharf

143

Cable Car Barn and Museum
See A to Z, Cable Cars

California Academy of Sciences
See A to Z, Golden Gate Park

California Historical Society
See A to Z, California Historical Society

California State Division of Mines Museum
See A to Z, Ferry Building

Cartoon Art Museum
665 Third Street
Open: Wed.–Fri. 10am–5pm

Chinatown Wax Musem. See A to Z, Chinatown

Exploratorium. See A to Z, Exploratorium

Friends of Photography
See A to Z, Friends of Photography

Haas-Lilienthal House
See A to Z, Haas-Lilienthal House

J. D. Randall Junior Museum (children's zoo)
199 Museum Way/Roosevelt Avenue
Open: Mon.–Fri. 10am–5pm

J. L. Magnus Memorial Museum (Jewish life)
University of California at Berkeley
2911 Russell Street
Open: Sun.–Fri. 10am–4pm

Mexican Museum
See A to Z, Mexican Museum

Mission Dolores. See A to Z, Mission Dolores

Museo Italo-Americano
Fort Mason, Building C, Marina Boulevard, tel. 673–2200
Open: Wed.–Sun. noon–5pm
Exhibits illustrating the art, culture and history of Italians who have
emigrated to the USA

Musée Méchanique (Mechanical musical instruments and toys)
in Cliff House, 1090 Point Lobos Avenue
(at the western end of Sutro Heights Park)
Open: daily 9am–4pm

Museum of the City of San Francisco
See A to Z, Museum of the City of San Francisco

Museum of Money of the American West
See A to Z, Bank of California

National Maritime Museum
See A to Z, National Maritime Museum

Navy/Marine Corps/Coast Guard Museum
See A to Z, Navy/Marine Corps/Coast Guard Museum

Oakland Museum
See A to Z, Oakland Museum

Octagon House
See A to Z, Octagon House

Pioneer Hall
See A to Z, Pioneer Hall

San Francisco African-American Historical and Cultural Society
See A to Z, San Francisco African-American Historical and Cultural Society

San Francisco Crafts and Folk Art Museum
Fort Mason, Building A, Marina Boulevard, tel. 775–0990
Open: Tue.–Sun. 11am–5pm
Temporary exhibitions on various themes relating to contemporary society
and popular art.

San Francisco Fire Department Pioneer Memorial Museum
See A to Z, San Francisco Fire Department Pioneer Memorial Museum

Society of California Pioneers
See A to Z, Pioneer Hall

Wax Museum
See A to Z, Fisherman's Wharf

Wells Fargo History Room
See A to Z, Wells Fargo History Room

World of Oil
See A to Z, World of Oil

World Trade Center
See A to Z, Ferry Building

Music

San Francisco's already rich musical life was greatly enhanced in the autumn of 1980 by the opening of the Louise M. Davies Symphony Hall (see A to Z, Civic Center), which meant that the San Francisco Opera, the Symphony Orchestra and the San Francisco Ballet no longer had to share the War Memorial Opera House.

General

The San Francisco Opera was founded in 1923. Its director from 1958 to 1981 was the Viennese conductor Kurt Herbert Adler who, despite the brevity of the season (from September to December), earned for the Opera international acclaim by engaging singers of international reputation and putting on a host of US first performances. The present director is Lotfi Mansouri. There are now two seasons a year, in the spring and autumn.

San Francisco Opera

Founded in 1911 the San Francisco Symphony Orchestra realised a long-standing ambition when it moved into premises of its own – the newly-built Louise M. Davies Concert Hall – in September 1980. The orchestra presents a season of concerts from September through to the end of May. Its present conductor is Herbert Blomstedt

San Francisco Symphony Orchestra

The San Francisco Ballet, formed in 1932, is the oldest permanent ballet company in the USA. It has established a considerable reputation with its fine blend of traditional and modern choreography. Many internationally known artists are engaged to dance with the troupe which is presently under the direction of Helgi Tomasson.

San Francisco Ballet

Concerts   The Louise M. Davies Symphony Hall is the city's principal concert venue, but concerts are also staged by some colleges of the San Francisco State University (tel. 469–2141) as well as the San Francisco Conservatory of Music (tel. 564–8086) and Mills College in neighbouring Oakland. In addition the Chamber Symphony of San Francisco (392–4400) and the San Francisco Sinfonia (922–3434) present concert series of their own.

During the season there are also 20 or so dance events per month in and around San Francisco. Programmes are published in the weekend "San Francisco Examiner-Chronicle".

Theatre   See Theatre

Last-minute tickets   See Theatre

Newspapers and Periodicals

Local papers   San Francisco has two principal daily newspapers: the morning "San Francisco Chronicle", with offices at 925 Mission Street, tel. 777–1111; and the evening "San Francisco Examiner", with offices at 110 Fifth Street, tel. 777–2424.
    These two combine in bringing out a weekend edition called the "San Francisco Examiner-Chronicle".

Other English-language publications include:
The "San Francisco Post", with offices at 630 20th Street, Oakland, tel. 510–763–1120
The "San Francisco Bay Guardian Weekly", with offices at 520 Hampshire Street, tel. 255–3100.

In addition there are any number of publications in Chinese, French, German, Italian, Japanese, Yiddish, Korean, Portuguese, Russian and Spanish, though few of these are dailies.

Nightlife

As San Francisco's nightlife is a constantly changing scene it is best to obtain up the minute information by checking in the paper or telephoning in advance. Some venues only have live entertainment on certain nights of the week.

Jazz, rock, pop   Great American Music Hall, 859 O'Farrell Street, tel. 885–0750
Hotel Utah, 500 Fourth Street, tel. 421–8308 (rock)
Kennel Club, 628 Divisadero Street, tel. 931–1914 (reggae, rock)
Kimball's Jazz Line, 300 Grove Street, tel. 861–5585 (jazz)
Last Day Saloon, 406 Clement Street, tel. 387–6343 (rock)
Morty's, 1024 Kearny Street, tel. 686–MORT (country and western, rock)
Pier 23 Café, Embarcadero, tel. 362–5125 (Dixieland jazz)
Plough and Stars, 116 Clement Street, tel. 751–1122 (live Irish)
The Saloon, 1232 Grant Avenue, tel. 989–7666 (jazz, blues)
Sound of Music, 269 Jefferson Street, tel. 885–0787 (rock)
The Stone, 412 Broadway, tel. 547–1954

Discothèques   Camelot, 3231 Fillmore Street, tel. 567–4004
I Beam, 1748 Haight Street, tel. 668–6006
Palladium, 1031 Kearny Street, tel. 434–1308
Rockin Robins, 1840 Haight Street, tel. 221–1960

Nightspots on Broadway (North Beach)

Opening Times

See Business hours

Passports and Visas

See Travel documents

Postal Services

The US Post Office is responsible only for mail services (US Mail), including money transfer. Telephone and cable (telegram) services are operated by private telephone companies (see Telephone).

Letters within the United States: 29 cents for the first ounce (28g), 23 cents for each additional ounce; postcards 14 cents.
   Airmail letters to Europe: 50 cents for the first half ounce (14g), 45 cents for each additional half ounce; postcards 40 cents; aerograms 40 cents.
   Stamps are best bought at a post office, a surcharge being applied to stamps from e.g. hotel automats.

Postal rates

Main Post Office
Seventh Street, corner of Market Street
Open 24 hours

Post offices

Rather more convenient are the post offices located in the basement of Macy's department store in Union Square and at 130 Sutter Street (open: Mon.–Fri. 9.30am–5.30pm, Sat. 9.30–1pm).

147

Programme of Events

Stamps	Outside business hours stamps are only available from coin automats (small change required).
Poste restante	Poste restante mail should be marked "General Delivery". It has to be collected from the Main Post Office.
Zip code	The zip code is a five-figure post code preceded by the two letter abbreviation for the particular state: e.g. San Francisco, CA 94100.
Letter-boxes	Mailboxes are blue in colour, with "US Mail" in white lettering.
Telephone	See entry

Programme of Events

A programme of events for the coming week appears in the "San Francisco Examiner-Chronicle", published each weekend.

Public Holidays

As elsewhere in the United States, San Francisco observes relatively few public holidays. Even then, apart from Thanksgiving Day, Easter Sunday, Christmas Day and New Year's Day, many businesses remain open. Banks, the Stock Exchange, administrative offices and schools do however close. There is no extra day's holiday at Christmas or Easter.

Religious festivals excepted, the dates of most public holidays apart from Independence Day are fixed annually. Usually the Monday immediately before or after the official holiday is chosen, so as to create a long weekend.

Official public holidays
New Year's Day (January 1st); Washington's Birthday (Monday before February 22nd); Easter Sunday; Memorial or Decoration Day (May 30th or the last Monday in May); Independence Day (July 4th); Labor Day (1st Monday in September); Columbus Day (October 12th or 2nd Monday in October); Veterans' Day (November 11th; in remembrance of those who died in the First World War); Thanksgiving Day (4th Thursday in November); Christmas Day (December 25th).

Public transportation (local services)

No smoking
Smoking is banned on all local public transport systems.

MUNI
Buses, trams, metro
The network of 57 bus routes operated by MUNI (the San Francisco Municipal Railway), provides the principal means of transport in the inner city. Buses operate from 6am to midnight, but on routes J, K, L, M, N, 14, 15, 22, 25 (in lieu of 47 and 30), 31, 38 and 41 there is a 24–hour service.

The current basic fare is 85 cents (seniors and tourists 15 cents); this allows two changes of route within a 90 minute period. Tickets are transferable between the different elements of the MUNI system including the Market Street trams (which run on Sundays only) and the MUNI Metro (weekdays). The correct fare must be tendered, no change being given.

MUNI day passes valid for all trams, buses and cable cars are also available (one-day $6; three-day $10; seven consecutive days $15). One-day passes only can be bought from ticket machines, otherwise passes are available from various MUNI outlets.

Pass holders also qualify for half-price admission to many museums and other similar attractions.

Tickets cost $2 and are valid for 2 hours.   Cable cars

The one-day MUNI pass costing $6 (see above) is available from ticket   Day pass
machines at cable car terminuses.

For further information dial 673–MUNI.   Information

A full bus timetable is printed at the beginning of "Yellow Pages", a copy of   Bus timetable
which is found in almost every hotel bedroom.

BART stands for Bay Area Rapid Transit, a subway and surface rail system   **BART**
linking San Francisco with communities on the east side of San Francisco
Bay. Opened in 1974 it extends north as far as Richmond, east as far as
Concord and south as far as Fremont, operating daily from 6am (Sunday
9am) to midnight.

BART has 34 stations, eight of them in San Francisco – Main and Market,   BART stations
Montgomery and Market, Powell and Market, Eighth Street and Market,
Sixteenth Street and Mission, Bosworth and San José, Geneva and San
José, Daly City.

Fares depend on length of journey.   Fares
   Ticket automats near the turnstiles take nickels, dimes and quarters (5, 10
and 25 cent coins) as well as $1 and $5 banknotes (change is given). Tickets
are then fed into a slot at the turnstile, which returns them stamped with a
code.
   At the end of the journey tickets are again fed into the turnstile slot. If not
fully used they will be returned and can go towards the next ride. In the case

Cable cars – part of the San Francisco experience

San Francisco Bay ferry – now just a nostalgic relic

of underpayment a sign "Underpaid Go To Adfare" lights up. The Adfare machine indicates how much is owing.

Excursion ticket

For $2.60 tourists can purchase an excursion ticket enabling the holder to ride anywhere on the 66 mile/107km network with its 34 stations for anything up to three hours. No exits are allowed at stations en route and the trip must end at the station where it began.

For information call 788–BART at any time.

Lost property

The BART lost property office is in the station at Twelfth Street and City Center in Oakland. It is open Mon.–Fri. noon–6pm (tel. 510–465–4100).

Ferries

Before the bridges over the Bay were built and the BART line was opened, ferries were the primary link between San Francisco on one side of the Bay and Marin County, Oakland, etc. on the other. Nowadays they have ceased to be of any major importance.

Ferry boat services still depart several times a day to Sausalito and Larkspur (from the right-hand side of the Ferry Building – see A to Z – when facing the Bay) and to Tiburon (left-hand side).

In the summer months a ferry service also operates from Pier 43½ to Tiburon and Angel Island. From Pier 41 there is a year-round ferry to Alcatraz.

For exact times of departure call:
332–6600 for Sausalito and Larkspur
788–1880 for Tiburon and Angel Island
546–2805 for Alcatraz

Radio and Television

Radio stations rarely transmit live programmes, most of them relying on tapes and records, etc. Some specialise in classical, jazz or rock music, while others are aimed at particular ethnic groups; yet others broadcast 24–hour news. There is a choice of some 30 stations of which those listed below together with their frequencies are a selection:

Radio stations

KCBS 740kHz (news only)
KSFO 560kHz
KFRC 610kHz (mainly rock music)
KNBR 680kHz
KGO 810kHz (news and live current affairs)
KNEW 910kHz (mainly country and western music)
KABL 960kHz (light music)
KIQI 1010kHz
KKHI 1550kHz (classical music)
KEST 1450kHz (religious, foreign language and live current affairs programmes)

There are eight TV stations, schedules for which are published in the daily and weekend papers (see Newspapers and periodicals).

Television

04 KRON, NBC
05 KPIX, CBS/Westinghouse Broadcasting
07 KGO, ABC
09 KOED, PBS (Public Broadcasting; no commercials)
02 KTVU, Fox Broadcasting (from Oakland)
11 KNTV, ABC (from San José)
14 KBHK, Fields Communications Corporation
20 KEMO, Crosby Productions

Rail and Bus Services

Railroads (railways) play such a small part in US long-distance transportation nowadays that visitors to San Francisco are unlikely to travel by train unless using the commuter rail services to the suburbs. These are operated by Southern Pacific which at one time was the most important of the private rail companies serving the city. The Southern Pacific terminal in San Francisco is at Fourth and Townsend Streets.

Rail

Those long-distance rail services which do survive (e.g. to Los Angeles, the Midwest and the North) depart not from San Francisco but from Oakland. They are operated by Amtrak, the heavily subsidised American national railroad corporation which (with some exceptions) leases its stations, track and rolling stock from the private rail companies.

Shuttle buses transport passengers from the San Francisco Transbay Terminal (Mission and First Streets, tel. 1–800–872–7245) to the Amtrak station in Oakland.

Shuttle service

Amtrak-appointed agents in the UK include:

UK agents

Albany Travel, 190 Deansgate, Manchester, tel. (0161) 833 0202
Compass, 9 Grosvenor Gardens, London SW1H 0BH, tel. (0171) 828 4111
Destination Marketing, York Road, London SW11 3TW, tel. (0171) 978 5212
Thistle Air, Bank Street, Kilmarnock, Ayrshire, tel. (01563) 71159

CalTrain: local service between San Francisco and San José
Fourth and Townsend Streets
Tel. 1–800–558–8661

CalTrain

151

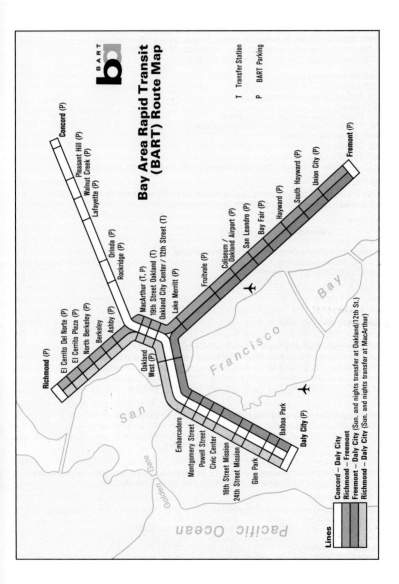

Bay Area Rapid Transit (BART) Route Map

Lines

Concord – Daly City
Richmond – Freemont
Freemont – Daly City (Sun. and nights transfer at Oakland/12th St.)
Richmond – Daly City (Sun. and nights transfer at MacArthur)

T   Transfer Station
P   BART Parking

Buses are considerably more important than rail for both local and long-distance travel.

SamTrans (routes south)
Transbay Terminal
Mission and First Streets, tel. 1–800–660–4BUS

AC Transit (routes north-east)
Transbay Terminal
Mission and First Streets, tel. 839–2882

Golden Gate Transit (to Marin and Sonoma Counties):
Market and Seventh Streets, tel. 332–6600

Greyhound
425 Mission Street/First Street, tel. 558–6789

Greyhound International, 14/16 Cockspur Street, London SW1, tel. (0171) 839 5591
Trailways, Balfour House, 590 Uxbridge Road, Hayes, Middlesex UB4 0RY, tel. (0181) 561 4656

The bus companies standardly offer special reductions (e.g. the "See America" bus pass) allowing unlimited travel throughout the USA for a specific period. This is considerably less expensive than buying tickets for each individual journey.

Rent-a-car

There is really no need to rent a car for getting about San Francisco. Most places can be reached on foot and driving in a city with 43 hills can present problems, particularly when it comes to parking on the steeply sloping streets where resident San Franciscans are at a distinct advantage over others. The principal factor however is the excellent public transport system: virtually everywhere in San Francisco is accessible, even if it means the occasional transfer. If speed is of the essence there are always taxis – available if the rooflight is on – which can be hailed from the sidewalk.

Renting a car is definitely worth while for excursions outside the city or if heading for Southern California or other parts of the United States.

A valid driving licence is essential (British licences are acceptable, as are those of certain other countries). Payment is best made by internationally recognised credit card (Visa, Mastercard, Eurocard); cash customers may be asked for a substantial deposit.

There is at present no standardly agreed age limit; some car hire firms stipulate 25 years, others 21. Most will accept younger drivers but charge an increased rate. If in doubt obtain clarification in advance from the company's main national booking office.

Most of the firms listed have offices at the airport, the first telephone number being that of the city office, the second of the airport office; those with prefix 1–800 are freephone numbers for use outside San Francisco only.

Alamo, 663 Geary Street, tel. 673–9696/1–800–327–9633 (for the airport also)
Avis, 675 Post Street, tel. 885–5011/877–6780/1–800–331–1212
Budget, 321 Mason Street, tel. 875–6850/877–4477/1–800–528–0700
Dollar, 364 O'Farrell Street, tel. 771–5300/1–800–800–4000

Parking made difficult on the slopes of San Francisco

Hertz, 433 Mason Street, tel. 771–2200/1–800–654–3131
National, 531 Sutter Street, tel. 474–5300/877–4745/1–800–328–4567
Pacific, 301 Mason Street, tel. 771–5300/692–2611
Thrifty, 299 Ellis Street, tel. 673–6675/1–800–367–2277

Charges

As a general rule car hire is cheaper in the USA than in Europe. Be sure to call up more than one rental company to compare rates. Sometimes there are special budget rates, especially for week-long rentals. Some firms charge mileage on top of the basic rental while others give a certain amount of free mileage. Returning the car to a company branch elsewhere may incur an additional charge. It is usually best to book a hire car in advance in Europe before setting off for the States.

Restaurants

General

San Francisco has an unbelievable number of restaurants ("Yellow Pages" lists more than 1800 but there are about 3500 in all) and an astonishing variety of national cuisines.

Besides Chinese, Japanese, French, Italian and fish restaurants, not to mention the countless places serving typical American food, visitors have the opportunity to sample Moroccan, Brazilian, Peruvian, Vietnamese, Korean and many other foreign dishes. In Chinatown (where one or two Japanese restaurants have also appeared) it is possible to eat extremely well, relatively cheaply.

San Francisco is particulary famous for its many seafood restaurants. In addition to a great variety of the more usual types of fish, shellfish and crustaceans, numerous dishes are prepared from the local delicacy abalone (a kind of edible mollusc).

A restaurant meal is an ideal opportunity to try the excellent California red and white wines.

Table reservations are required, especially in expensive restaurants and at weekends. Except in coffee shops customers are always escorted to their tables. Sales tax of 8% is added to the bill and a tip (see Tipping) should be given. Almost all restaurants accept credit cards (American Express, Mastercard and Visa, and sometimes also Diners Club and Carte Blanche).

See Business hours

Opening times

The type of cuisine is indicated by letters after the name of each restaurant, as follows:

Cuisine

A = American	I = Italian
Ar = Armenian	In = Indian
Ch = Chinese	J = Japanese
Co = Continental	Mc = Moroccan
F = French	Me = Mexican
Fi = Fish	Pol = Polynesian
G = German	R = Russian
Gr = Greek	Sp = Spanish
H = Hungarian	St = Steak
Hw = Hawaiian	Sw = Swiss

Cathay House (Ch), 718 California Street, tel. 982–3388
Empress of China (Ch), 838 Grant Avenue, tel. 434–1345
Four Seas (Ch), 731 Grant Avenue, tel. 397–5577
Imperial Palace (Ch), 919 Grant Avenue, tel. 989–8188
Kan's (Ch), 708 Grant Avenue, tel. 982–2388
Yamato Sukiyaki (J), 717 California Street, tel. 397–3456

Restaurants in Chinatown

Acquerello (I), 1722 Sacramento Street, tel. 567–5432 (expensive)
Bardelli's (Co), 243 O'Farrell Street, tel. 982–0243
Brasserie Chambord (F), 152 Kearny Street, tel. 434–3688
Cypress Club (A), 500 Jackson Street, tel. 296–8555 (expensive)
Donatello (I), Post and Mason Street, tel. 441–7182 (expensive)
Fleur de Lys (F), 777 Sutter Street, tel. 673–7779 (expensive)
Iron Horse (I), 19 Maiden Lane, tel. 382–8133
La Mère Duquesne (F), 101 Shannon Alley, tel. 776–7600
Le Central (F), 453 Bush Street, tel. 391–2233 (expensive)
Lefty O'Doul's (A), 333 Geary Street, tel. 982–8900
Lehr's Greenhouse (H), 740 Sutter Street, tel. 474–6478
The Magic Pan (A), 341 Sutter Street, tel. 788–7397
Marrakech (Mo), 417 O'Farrell Street, tel. 776–6717
Masa's (F), 648 Bush Street, tel. 989–7154 (expensive)
Omar Khayyam's (Ar), 196 O'Farrell Street, tel. 781–1010
Salmagundi (Co), 442 Geary Street, tel. 441–0894 (self service)
Sam's Grill (Fi), 347 Bush Street, tel. 421–0594
Tadich Grill (Fi), 240 California Street, tel. 391–2373
Trader Vic's (Pol), 20 Cosmo Place, tel. 776–2232 (very expensive)

Downtown

Four Seasons Clift Hotel, 495 Geary Street
  French Room (Co), Tel. 775–4700 (very expensive)
Grand Hyatt San Francisco, 345 Stockton Street
  Club 36 (Co), on the 3rd floor, tel. 398–1234
  Plaza Restaurant (fish/I/A), tel. 398–1234
San Francisco Hilton, Mason Street/O'Farrell Street
  Café on the Square (A), tel. 771–1400
  Cityscape (A), on the 46th floor, tel. 776–0215
Sir Francis Drake Hotel, Sutter Street/Powell Street
  Crusty's Sourdough (A), tel. 392–7755
  Starlite Roof (Co). tel. 392–7755 (lunch only, dancing in the evenings)

Hotel restaurants downtown

Restaurants

Westin St Francis Hotel, Union Square
St Francis Grill (Fi), tel. 956–7777
Victor's (F), tel. 956–7777
Oz (cocktails, dancing 9pm–2am)

Financial district
Carnelian Room (F), 555 California Street, tel. 433–7500
Ernie's (F), 847 Montgomery Street, tel. 397–5969 (very expensive)
Harbor Village Restaurant (Ch), 4 Embarcadero Center, tel. 781–8833
Jack's (F), 615 Sacramento Street, tel. 986–9854
Palio d'Asti (I), 640 Sacramento Street, tel. 395–9800
Schroeder's (G), 240 Front Street, tel. 421–4778

Hotel restaurants in the financial district
Hyatt Regency San Francisco, 5 Embarcadero Center
Hugo's (Co), tel. 788–1234 (very expensive)
Equinox (A), on the 18th floor, tel. 788–1234
Market Place (A), tel. 788–1234

Fisherman's Wharf
Castagnola's (Fi), 286 Jefferson Street, tel. 776–5015
Franciscan (Fi), Pier 43 1–2, tel. 382–7733
Pompei's Grotto (Fi), 340 Jefferson Street, tel. 776–9265
Scoma's (Fi), Pier 47, tel. 771–4383

Hotel restaurant
Sheraton at Fisherman's Wharf, 2500 Mason Street
Grand Exhibition (A), tel. 982–5536 (very expensive)

Ghirardelli Square
Gaylord (In), 900 North Point, tel. 771–8822
Mandarin (Ch), 900 North Point, tel. 673–8812
Paprikas Fono (H), 900 North Point, tel. 441–1223

North Beach
Beethoven (G), 1201 Powell Street at Union Street tel. 391–4488

Restaurant at Fisherman's Wharf

Big Four (A), 1075 California Street, tel. 771–1140 (very expensive) Nob Hill
Brandy Ho's on Broadway 8 (Ch), 450 Broadway
Fournou's Ovens (F), 905 California Street, tel. 989–1910 (very expensive)

Fairmont Hotel, California Street/Mason Street Hotel
   The Tonga (Po), tel. 772–5211 restaurants on
   The Squire (F/Co), tel. 772–5211 (very expensive) Nob Hill
   Crown Restaurant (buffet), on the 29th floor, tel. 772–5131
   Bella Voce (A), tel. 772–5199 (open 24 hours)
Ritz Carlton, 600 Stockton Street
   The Dining Room (F), tel. 296–7465
   The Restaurant (A), tel. 296–7465
Sheraton Palace, 2 New Montgomery Street
   Garnier Court (Co), tel. 392–8600 (very expensive)
   Kyo-Ya (J), tel. 392–8600 (expensive)

Chic's Place (Fi), Pier 39, tel. 421–2442 Pier 39
Dante's Sea Catch (I/Fi), Pier 39, tel. 421–5778
Neptune's Palace, (Fi), Pier 39, tel. 434–2260

Julius's Castle (Co), 1541 Montgomery Street, tel. 362–3042 (very Telegraph Hill
expensive)

Green's at Fort Mason (Building A), tel. 771–6222 (the most interesting of Fort Mason
San Francisco's vegetarian restaurants, run by the San Francisco Zen
Center).

Shopping

See Business hours Opening times

Department stores

San Francisco has relatively few department stores. Among the best-
known are:

Emporium, 835 Market Street, tel. 764–2222
Gump's, 250 Post Street, tel. 982–1616
Macy's, Union Square, tel. 397–3333
I. Magnin, Union Square, tel. 362–2100
Neiman-Marcus, 150 Stockton Street, tel. 362–3900
Nordstrom, corner of Market and Fifth Streets, tel. 243–8500
Saks Fifth Avenue, 384 Post Street, tel. 986–4300

Most department stores open for business between 9 and 9.30am. Smaller Business hours
stores usually close around 5.30pm; most of the larger ones stay open until
9pm three to five days a week.

Shopping Centres

San Francisco's principal shopping centres today are the shopping and
restaurant complexes at Ghirardelli Square, The Anchorage, The Cannery
and Pier 39 (all located at Fisherman's Wharf – see entries in A to Z). Other
main shopping areas are at Jackson Square, in Cow Hollow, Union Square
and Chinatown. The newest centre is at 865 Market Street opposite the
cable car terminus.

Shopping with a difference – the Neiman-Marcus department store

Speciality shops

For reasons of space only a few of the city's many shops can be mentioned here; most of those listed are in downtown San Francisco.

Bookshops
: See entry

Bread
: Sourdough bread has been baked in the city since the very early days, the recipe having been introduced in 1849 by an immigrant baker from France. The Boudin bakery and shops, still owned by the same family, are on Fisherman's Wharf but sourdough bread is sold almost everywhere in San Francisco including at the airport.

Camera shops
: Brooks Cameras, 45 Kearny Street and 243 Montgomery Street
Camera Boutique, 250 Kearny Street
Discount Camera and Video, 33 Kearny Street

Flowers
: Hoogasian, 250 Post Street (at Gump's), 480 Sutter Street and 1640 Lombard Street
Kalman and Belli, 28 Third Street/corner of Market Street
Sheridan and Bell, 90 Lombard Street
Flower stalls are a common sight around Union Square, Market Street, etc.

Gentlemen's fashions
: Ariston, 349 Sutter Street
Rochester Big and Tall Clothing, Mission Street and Third Street
The Town Squire, 1318 Polk Street
Wilkes Bashford, 375 Sutter Street

Gift shops
: Cost Plus, 2552 Taylor Street (Fisherman's Wharf)
The Mole Hole, 1895 Union Street
Only in San Francisco, Pier 39 (Fisherman's Wharf)

Sour Dough – a San Francisco speciality

Aurum Gallery, 116 Maiden Lane	Jewellery
Boring & Company, 140 Geary Street	
Carrera y Carrera Boutique, 865 Market Street (S. F. Shopping Center)	
Da Vinci Fine Jewelry Center, 170 Powell Street	
Pearl Empire, 127 Geary Street	
Tiffany's, 350 Post Street	
Jessica McClintock, 353 Sutter Street	Ladies' fashions
Lanz, 45 Grant Avenue	
I. Magnin, Geary Street and Stockton Street (Union Square)	
Victoria's Secret, 395 Sutter Street	
Brooks Brothers, 201 Post Street	Ladies' and
Neiman-Marcus, 150 Stockton Street	gentlemen's
Saks Fifth Avenue, 384 Post Street	fashions

The Napa Valley Winery Exchange, 415 Taylor Street (tel. 771–2887), has a large selection of Californian wines and champagnes. Less well known vineyards are represented as well as the leading ones. Wine

Sightseeing Tours

A great variety of sightseeing tours are available by bus, boat, helicopter and on foot. Hotels keep a stock of brochures and will make the necessary bookings. Except for boat tours other than to Alcatraz, it is advisable to book at least a day in advance.

San Francisco is particularly suited to exploration on foot; there are any number of guided walking tours. Tours on foot

Sightseeing Tours

A. M. Walks, tel. 928–5965
A 2-hour walk in the very early morning led by author John McCarroll who talks about San Francisco's notorious past. Takes in the streets and buildings around Union Square, Chinatown and the Barbary Coast. Advance booking essential.

Chinatown Discovery Tours, tel. 982–8839
A behind-the-scenes tour of Chinatown with visits to a "secret" Buddhist temple, an unusual herb shop, food markets and museums; ends in pleasant fashion with a meal in a traditional Chinese restaurant. Advance booking essential.

Chinese Cultural Center, tel. 966–1822
Groups only and by prior arrangement: a walk through Chinatown with a dim-sum lunch.
    Individuals and groups by prior arrangement: a walk through Chinatown, Saturdays at 2pm.
    Tours leave from the Chinese Cultural Center, 750 Kearny Street (second floor of the Holiday Inn).

Helen's Walk Tour, tel. 510–524–4544
A 4-hour tour encompassing Victorian houses, Coit Tower, sights in North Beach and the interesting murals in Mission District south of Market Street. Advance booking essential.

Heritage Walks, tel. 441–3004
Sundays only, 12.30pm and occasionally in the late afternoon: a walk arranged by the Foundation for San Francisco's Heritage focusing on the city's history, and cultural institutions in the Pacific Heights district.

Near Escapes, tel. 921–1392
An unusual programme of "behind-the-scenes" tours; not sightseeing in the ordinary sense, but something special – a backstage view of a luxury hotel, Chinatown as it once was, San Francisco's railroads yesterday and today, etc. Also available a 1½ hour commentary on cassette for those wishing to follow the Scenic Route in their own car. Address: P.O. Box 3005, San Francisco CA 94119.

Roger's Walking Tours, tel. 415–742–9611
9.30am–12.30pm; includes a cable car ride and buffet lunch in the Fairmont Hotel.

San Francisco Discovery Walks, tel. 673–2894
Walks in lesser known parts of the city. Call the number for further information.

City Guides, tel. 557–4266
Free tours of various city districts organised by the Friends of San Francisco Public Library. Telephone for information about times and meeting places (printed schedules also available from the main Public Library building in the Civic Center – see A to Z – and all branch libraries).

Car tour

49 Mile Scenic Drive
A 49 mile/79km sightseeing drive marked by blue, white and orange seagull signs. Best begun from the Civic Centre (see A to Z), it takes in practically all San Francisco's major sights.

Bus tours

Cat Tours, tel. 826–1155
A choice of four minibus tours (max. 14 seats): San Francisco; Sausalito and Muir Woods; San Francisco and Muir Woods; Monterey and Carmel. Hotel pick up if required.

Golden Gate Tours, tel 788–5775
Daily: 3-hour city tour dep. 9.30am (also 2pm in summer); 3½-hour tour to Sausalito and Muir Woods dep. 2pm (also 9.30am in summer). Whole day tour to Monterey and Carmel, Tue., Thur. and Sat. dep. 9.30am. Whole day tour of the Wine Country, daily, individuals dep. 9am, groups 9.30am. Hotel pick up.

Gray Line, tel. 588–9411
Daily tours leaving from the Gray Line Terminal at First and Mission Streets. Six 3½-hour city tours dep. 9am, 10am, 11am, 1pm, 2pm and 3pm; three city tours combined with a boat trip dep. 9am, 10am and 11am; two "San Francisco by Night" tours dep. 7pm (includes a meal in a Chinatown restaurant) and 8pm.

Great Pacific Tours, tel. 626–4499
Daily 3½-hour city tours (dep. 9.30am and 2.45pm, also 3.45pm in summer). Muir Woods and Sausalito, May–Oct. daily, otherwise Wed.–Sun., dep. 9.30am and 1.30pm. Monterey and Carmel, May–Oct. daily, otherwise Wed.–Sun., dep. 8am. Hotel pick up.

Streets of San Francisco Tours, tel. 1–800–BUS-4YOU
San Francisco; Sausalito and Muir Woods; San Francisco, Sausalito, Muir Woods combined; Napa Valley; Monterey and Carmel; Yosemite. Depart daily from Union Square. Hotel pick up.

See Boat tours | Boat trips

Commodore Helicopter Tours, tel. 332–4482 | Helicopter tours
Operate daily 9.30am–sunset from Pier 43, Fisherman's Wharf; 4-minute flights over the Bay at a height of 650ft/200m.

San Francisco Helicopter Tours, tel. 510–635–4500
Flights over the Bay, Napa Valley, Monterey peninsula, etc.

Boat and helicopter tours are weather permitting; if in doubt call the companies concerned. | **N.B.**

Tours to places outside San Francisco

All the bus companies operating city tours also run day-trips to places outside San Francisco. These include:

Sausalito, Muir Woods and San Francisco Bay: Golden Gate, Gray, Great Pacific
Napa and Sonoma Valley "Wine Country": City, Gray, Great Pacific
Monterey, 17 Mile Drive and Carmel: Golden Gate, Gray, Great Pacific
Yosemite National Park: Gray (daily, dep. 6.40am).

Sport

San Francisco Giants: April to end of September, Candlestick Park, 8 miles/13km south of San Francisco off Bayshore Freeway (information: tel. 467–8000 or 982–9400) | Baseball
Oakland Athletics: April to end of September in Oakland Coliseum (information: tel. 510–638–0500).

San Francisco 49ers: Sundays from August to December, Candlestick Park, 8 miles/13km south of San Francisco off Bayshore Freeway (information: tel. 468–2249). | Football

Golf	San Francisco has four public golf courses: Harding Park Course, Lake Merced Boulevard, tel. 664–4690 Lincoln Park Course, 34th Avenue and Clement Street, tel. 221–9911 Golden Gate Park Course, 47th Avenue and Fulton Street, tel. 751–8987 Sharp Park Course, Highway 1, in Pacifica, tel. 355–2862
Race-course	Bay Meadows Race Track: 20 miles/32km south of San Francisco in San Mateo, between Bayshore Freeway and El Camino Real. Racing on 200 days in the year (information: tel. 574–7223).
Riding	In Golden Gate Park: Golden Gate Park Stables, Kennedy Drive and 34th Avenue, tel. 668–7360.
Tennis	San Francisco has more than 100 tennis courts; with the exception of the 21 courts in Golden Gate Park, all are free; for information and booking call 415–4800. San Francisco Tennis Club, 645 Fifth Street: a private club with twelve indoor and sixteen outdoor courts available to visitors on payment of a fee (tel. 777–9000).

Taxis (Cabs)

General	San Francisco is well-served by cabs. They are best ordered by phone; hailing a cab in the street seldom meets with success.
Fares	Minimum fare for the first mile/1.6km is $1.90, then $1.50 for each additional mile. Waiting time is charged at 20 cents a minute. Since journeys in San Francisco are generally speaking short (except to those parts of the city next to the sea), most cab rides are relatively inexpensive. The fare from the airport to downtown San Francisco is about $25 (plus tip).
Telephone bookings	Firms normally operating a 24–hour service include:

Checker Cabs	626–2345
City Cab	468–7200
De Soto Cab	673–1414
Luxor Cab	282–4141
Veterans' Taxi Cab	552–1300
Yellow Cab	626–2345

Telegrams

See Telephone

Telephone

See also Useful telephone numbers at a glance.

Dialling codes	San Francisco: 415. The East Bay counties of Alameda and Contra Costa, encompassing Oakland, Berkeley, Concord, Pleasanton and Livermore: 510 To the United Kingdom: 011–44. To Canada: as for long-distance calls within the United States (i.e. dial 0 followed by the local dialling code). Freephone numbers: 1–800.
Local calls	Local calls from coin-operated telephones cost 25 cents (hotels charge double or even treble the standard rate).

Since coin-operated telephones do not accept coins larger than 25 cents, directly dialled long-distance (and in particular international calls) cannot easily be made from them.

Nor can long-distance calls be made from post offices (see Postal Services). Reversed charge (collect) calls can however be made from coin-operated telephones via the operator.

The cost per minute of a call to Europe is $1.42 between 6pm and 7am, $2.37 between 7am and 1pm, and $1.78 between 1pm and 6pm (plus tax). The cost of a three-minute call dialled direct is between $12.60 and $7.05.

Calls can also be made using an AT & T Card, available to holders of a Diners Club or Visa (Banco de Santander) credit card or US bank account. The call is connected by an AT & T operator in New York (using Touch Tone equipment); the card number is typed in and the cost of the call is then charged to the holder's account.

    AT & T publish an "International Telephone Guide" explaining the some-what complicated procedure. Hotels usually have a copy.

Telegrams generally have to be telephoned; there are very few telegraph offices where they can be handed in.

Television

See Radio and television

Theatre

The American Conservatory Theatre (450 Geary Street, near Union Square) ranks among the finest provincial theatres in the United States. This perma-nent theatre company puts on a balanced selection of drama, tragedy and comedy, with about ten new productions every season. Because the Geary Theater, its home for many years, was badly damaged in the earthquake, the company now performs at the Stage Door Theater (420 Mason Street) and the Theater on the Square (450 Post Street). Call 749–2228 for pro-gramme details.

    The famous San Francisco Mime Troup performs in the open-air in parks during the summer and indoors in various theatres during the winter (tel. 285–1717).

The following little theatres stage their own productions:
Eureka Theater, 2730 Sixteenth Street, tel. 558–9898
Julian Theater, 777 Valencia Street, tel. 626–8986

Other theatres, with a wide spectrum of programmes, include:
Curran Theater, 445 Geary Street, tel. 474–3800
Golden Gate Theater, Golden Gate and Taylor Streets, tel. 474–3800
Magic Theater, Fort Mason, Building D, tel. 441–8822
Mason Street Theater, 340 Mason Street, tel. 981–0260
Marines Memorial Theater, 325 Mason Street, tel. 771–6900
Orpheum Theater, 1192 Market Street, tel. 474–3800
Lamplighters Music Theater, 2350 Turk Street, tel. 752–7755
Zephyr Theater, 25 Van Ness Avenue, tel. 861–6655

Theatre programme information is published in the daily and weekend press (see Newspapers and periodicals).

Time

Opera, concerts and ballet	See Music.
Half-price tickets	The STBS office on the Stockton Street side of Union Square (open: Tue.–Sat. noon–7.30pm) frequently has concert, ballet and theatre tickets at half-price (cash only) on the day of performance. Enquiries to 433–STBS.

Time

San Francisco is on Pacific Standard Time which is 3 hours behind Eastern Standard Time and 8 hours behind Greenwich Mean Time.

Daylight Saving Time (Pacific Standard Time + 1 hour) is in force from the first Sunday in April to the last Sunday in October.

Tipping

Service charges are very seldom added to bills in the United States so tipping is common practice.

Hotel	Bellboys are usually tipped 50 cents for each item of baggage.
	    It is normal to leave the room maid a tip of 50 cents ($1 for a double room) on departure.
	    A doorman who summons a cab will expect between 50 cents and $1.

Restaurants	The usual tip – always left on the table – is 15% of the bill not including the 8% sales tax. In the better class restaurants the maître d'hôtel (head waiter) should also be tipped.
Cabs	Cab drivers expect 15% of the metered fare, perhaps slightly more for short journeys.
Barbers and hairdressers	The usual tip is 15%.
Shoeshine	A 25 cent tip is the norm.

Tourist Information

In the UK	The United States Travel and Tourism Administration (USTTA) has offices in countries throughout the world. It has a London office (P.O. Box 1EN, London W1A 1EN) but is best contacted by telephone on (0171) 495 4466. It supplies a useful information pack, including a Holiday Planner, a map of the United States, visa information and USA Travelfax.

In San Francisco	San Francisco Convention and Visitors Bureau, 201 Third Street, Suite 900, San Francisco CA 94103, tel. (415) 974–6900.
	    (Free maps, brochures, accommodation listings and events schedules.)
	
	The Bureau's Visitor Center (tel. 391–2000) is located in Hallidie Plaza at the intersection of Powell and Market Streets (lower level; nearest MUNI metro station: Powell Street).
	    Open: Mon.–Fri. 9am–5.30pm, Sat. 9am–3pm, Sun. 10am–2pm. Closed: Thanksgiving Day, Christmas Day and New Year's Day.
	
	Redwood Empire Association, 785 Market Street, San Francisco CA 94103, tel. (415) 543–8334. (Information on the entire California North Coast.)
	
	Chronicle Cityline is a free 24-hour telephone information service (news, weather, sports, business, trivia and more); tel. 777–6035.

International Visitors Center, 312 Sutter Street, San Francisco, tel. 986–1388. Open: Mon.–Fri. 9am–5pm (assistance for foreign visitors).

Travel Phone USA is a free nationwide multilingual tourist assistance and information service for visitors from abroad, tel. 1–800–255–3050.

Dial 391–1200

Day's events

Tel. 673–MUNI

City buses (MUNI)

Tel. 788–BART

BART

Travel Documents

Passports are required by all visitors to the United States except Canadian or British subjects resident in Canada or Bermuda and returning there from a visit to a country in North, Central or South America. British visitors must have a regular ten-year passport; the one-year British visitor's passport is not valid for the USA.

Visas are not required by Canadian citizens, nor by British citizens staying in the USA for less than 90 days and holding an onward ticket issued by a carrier who has agreed to participate in the no-visa programme. If in doubt about visa requirements call the US Embassy in London on (0171) 499 3443 (recorded information) or (0171) 499 7010.

Weather Reports

The periodic newscasts on radio and television (see entry) include updated weather reports and forecasts. Call 936–1212 for Bay Area weather.

Weights and Measures

1 inch=2.54cm	1 mm=0.039 in.	Length
1 foot=30.48cm	1cm=0.033ft	
1 yard=91.44cm	1 m=1.09yd	
1 mile=1.61km	1km=0.62 mile	

1 sq.in.=6.45 sq.cm	1 sq.cm=0.155 sq.in.	Area
1 sq.ft=9.288 sq.dm	1 sq.dm=0.108 sq.ft	
1 sq.yd=0.836 sq.m	1 sq.m=1.196 sq.yd	
1 sq.mile=2.589km	1km=0.386 sq.mile	
1 acre=0.405 hectare	1 hectare=2.471 acres	

1 cu.in.=16.386 cu.cm	1 cu.cm=0.061 cu.in.	Volume
1 cu.ft=28.32 cu.dm	1 cu.dm=0.035 cu.ft	
1 cu.yd=0.765 cu.m	1 cu.m=1.308 cu.yd	

The US gallon and other measures of capacity are smaller than the corresponding British (Imperial) measure; one US gallon equals 0.83 British gallon. The following metric equivalences are for the US units.

Liquid measure

1 gill=0.118 litre	1 litre=8.474 gills
1 pint=0.473 litre	1 litre=2.114 pints
1 quart=0.946 litre	1 litre=1.057 quarts
1 gallon=3.787 litres	1 litre=0.264 gallon

Youth Hostels

Weight	1 oz=28.35 g	100 g=3.527 oz
	1 lb=453.59 g	1 kg=2.205 lb
	1 cwt=45.359 kg	100 kg=2.206 cwt
	1 ton=0.907 tonne	1 tonne=1.103 tons

The US hundredweight is smaller than the British hundredweight (100 lb instead of 112 lb), and the US ton is the short ton of 2000 lb (as opposed to the British long ton of 2240 lb and the metric tonne of 1000 kg or 2204 lb). The metric equivalences given above are for the US units.

Temperature	Fahrenheit	Centigrade	Conversions
	0°	−18°	
	10°	−12°	°C = 5(°F − 32) ÷ 9
	20°	−5°	
	32°	0°	°F = (1·8 × °C) + 32
	50°	10°	
	68°	20°	Ratios
	86°	30°	°C : °F = 5 : 9
	95°	35°	°F : °C = 9 : 5

Youth Hostels

YMCA	YMCA Central Branch (100 r.), 220 Golden Gate Avenue, tel. 885–0460
	YMCA Embarcadero Branch (275 r.), 169 Steuart Street, tel. 392–2191
	YWCA Hotel (primarily for women), 620 Sutter Street, tel. 775–6500
Youth Hostels	San Francisco International Youth Hostel (165 b.), Fort Mason (Bay Street/ Van Ness Avenue), Building 240, tel. 771–7277
	Golden Gate Youth Hostel (60 b.), Sausalito, 941 Fort Barry, tel. 331–2777

Useful Telephone Numbers at a Glance

Airlines
  British Airways   1–800–247–9297
  PanAm   1–800–221–1111
  TWA   1–800–221–2000

Embassies/Consulates
  UK   981–3030
  Canada   495–6021

Emergency calls
  Medical emergency, Fire
    department, Police   911
  Ambulance   931–3900

Information
  Buses (long distance)
    Greyhound   433–1500
    Trailways   982–6400
  Buses (local)
    AC Transit   510–839–2882
    Airporter (to the airport)   673–2432
    Golden Gate Transit   332–6600
    Samtrans   1–800–660–4287
  Public transportation
    BART (Bay Area Rapid Transit) 788–BART
    MUNI (Municipal Railway
      Company)   673–MUNI
  Events
    San Francisco Convention and
      Visitors Bureau   974–6900
    The Bureau's Visitor Information
      Center   391–2000
    Redwood Empire Association   543–8334
    International Visitors Center   986–1388
    Travel Phone USA   1–800–225–3050
    Tourist Information   626–5500
    Day's Events   391–1200
    USSTA in the UK   (0171) 495 4466
    Weather forecast   936–1212
    Time   767–8900

Lost Property
  BART   510–465–4100

Rail services
  AMTRAK Transbay Terminal   1–800–872–7245
  Southern Pacific Railroad   495–4546
  Caltrain   1–800–558–8661

Telephone
  Information San Francisco   411
  California   555–1212
  Information USA   Area Code +
                      555–1212
  Information abroad   0 (operator)
  Dialling code for UK   011–44

Telegram   648–4100

Index

Imprint

102 illustrations, 10 special plans, 2 ground plans, 4 drawings, 1 transport map, 1 large city map at end of book

German text: Henry Marx
Editorial work: Baedeker, Stuttgart

General direction: Dr Peter Baumgarten, Baedeker Stuttgart

Cartography: Christoph Gallus, Hohberg-Niederschopfheim; Rand McNally & Co., Chicago, IL (city map)

Source of Illustrations: Drechsler-Marx (68), Fine Arts Museum of San Francisco (1), Historia (1), Messerschmidt (27), Ullstein (4), ZEFA-Benser (1)

Original English Translation: Babel Translations, Norwich

Revised text: Wendy Bell

Editorial work: Margaret Court

3rd English edition 1995

© Baedeker Stuttgart
Original German edition 1995

© 1995 Jarrold and Sons Ltd
English language edition worldwide

© 1995 The Automobile Association
United Kingdom and Ireland

Published in the United States by:
Macmillan Travel
A Simon & Schuster Macmillan Company
1633 Broadway
New York, NY 10019–6785

Macmillan is a registered trademark of Macmillan, Inc.

Distributed in the United Kingdom by the Publishing Division of the Automobile Association, Fanum House, Basingstoke, Hampshire RG21 2EA

Licensed user: Mairs Geographischer Verlag GmbH & Co., Ostfildern-Kemnat bei Stuttgart

The name *Baedeker* is a registered trademark

A CIP catalogue record of this book is available from the British Library

Printed in Italy by G. Canale & C.S.p.A – Borgaro T.se –Turin

ISBN 0–02–860667–1 US and Canada

Notes

Notes